beautiful
embroidered
quilts

INSPIRATIONS BOOKS

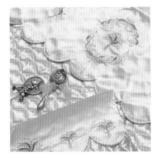

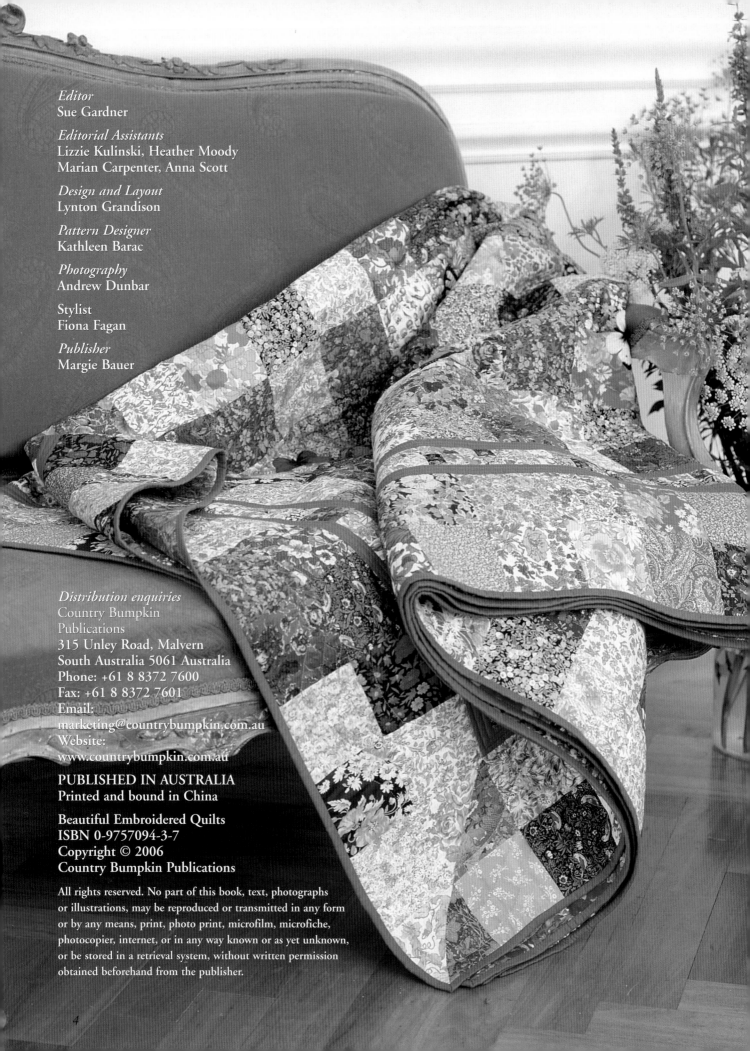

Editor
Sue Gardner

Editorial Assistants
Lizzie Kulinski, Heather Moody
Marian Carpenter, Anna Scott

Design and Layout
Lynton Grandison

Pattern Designer
Kathleen Barac

Photography
Andrew Dunbar

Stylist
Fiona Fagan

Publisher
Margie Bauer

Distribution enquiries
Country Bumpkin
Publications
315 Unley Road, Malvern
South Australia 5061 Australia
Phone: +61 8 8372 7600
Fax: +61 8 8372 7601
Email:
marketing@countrybumpkin.com.au
Website:
www.countrybumpkin.com.au

PUBLISHED IN AUSTRALIA
Printed and bound in China

Beautiful Embroidered Quilts
ISBN 0-9757094-3-7
Copyright © 2006
Country Bumpkin Publications

*In this world it is not what we take up, but what
we give up, that makes us rich.*

HENRY WARD BEECHER

The six glorious quilts featured in the following pages will take your breath away. Designed by six of Australia's most talented embroiderers, they combine the best of both quilting and embroidery. This fusion of quilting and embroidery as equal partners within a cloth creation sets a new emphasis for future quilters everywhere. It is one that can only add to the beauty and diversity of what can be achieved with a needle and thread.

I do hope you will love either reproducing these works of art, or alternatively, borrowing pieces from them to create your own masterpiece.

To ensure these projects are within the reach of anyone with a desire to create something beautiful from fabric, we have included easy to follow step-by-step instructions for every embroidery stitch and quilting technique that is needed to replicate these fabulous quilts.

Enjoy!

Sue

Sue Gardner

Sailor Bears
by Julie Graue

Snuggle up and dream of seaside adventures

with these cheeky little bears, dressed in their very best sailor shirts
and jaunty matching caps. Embroidered onto cream flannel with soft wool
threads, the bears are surrounded by borders of blue gingham,
highlighted with a line of bright red piping.

STITCHES AND TECHNIQUES

Back stitch, Fly stitch
Ghiordes knot, Granitos
Long and short stitch
Padded satin stitch
Satin stitch, Split stitch
Stem stitch
Piecing by machine
Hand quilting, Sashing

Did you know?

During the Spanish-American War, Sailors wore leggings called boots, which came to mean a Navy (or Marine) recruit. These recruits trained in 'boot' camps.

Requirements

Fabric

A = ivory Doctor's flannel
55cm x 100cm wide (21¾" x 39½")

B = large check gingham
1.5m x 112cm wide (1yd 23" x 44")

C = small check gingham
1m x 112cm wide (39½" x 44")

Embroidery threads

Appleton 2 ply crewel wool

D = 182 very light chocolate
x 2 skeins

E = 183 light chocolate x 2 skeins

F = 185 chocolate x 1 skein

G = 981 very light putty groundings
x 4 skeins

H = 991 cream x 1 skein

DMC Broder Médicis fine wool

I = blanc x 2 skeins

J = 8666 Christmas red x 2 skeins

K = 8799 medium delft x 3 skeins

L = 8800 pale delft x 2 skeins

Supplies

Wool batting 1m x 115cm wide
(39½" x 45¼")

Christmas red mini piping
3.8m (4yd 6")

Tracing paper

Fine black pen

Fine water-soluble fabric marker

Embroidery hoop 15cm (6") wide

Transparent quilting thread

No. 24 tapestry needle

Cutting Out

Cut nine blocks from the Doctor's flannel, each 26cm x 19.5cm wide (10¼" x 7⅝").

Cut out all other pieces following the instructions on the liftout pattern sheet.

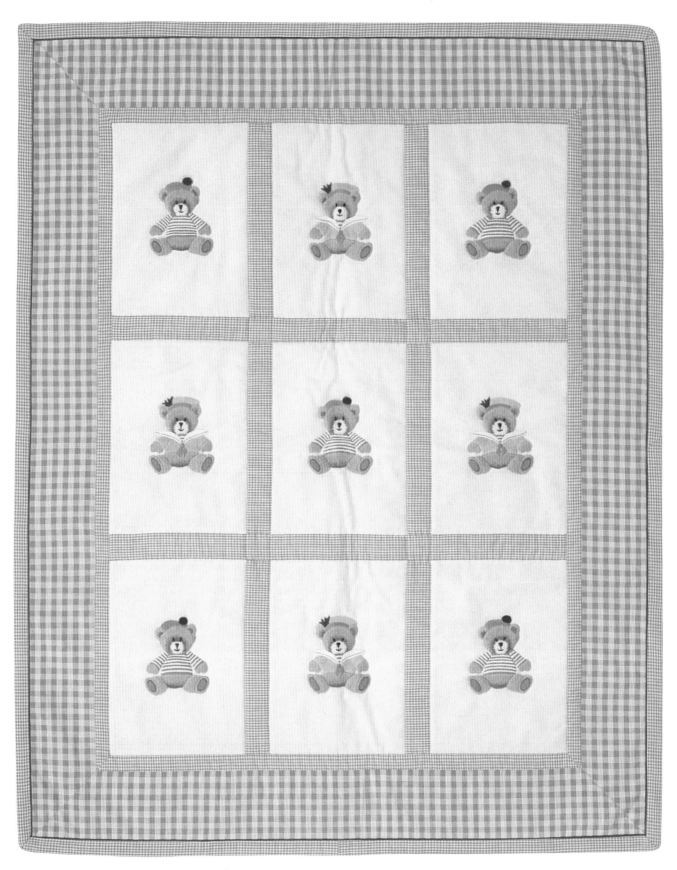

The quilt measures 103cm x 85cm wide (40⅝" x 33½").

Preparation for Embroidery

Transferring the designs

See the liftout pattern sheet for the embroidery designs.

Using the fine black pen, trace each embroidery design onto a separate piece of tracing paper. Tape the tracing of the bear in the striped top to a window or light box. With the right side of a block of Doctor's flannel facing you, centre it over the tracing. Tape in place. Using the water-soluble fabric marker, trace the design onto the fabric. Repeat the procedure four more times.

Tape the tracing of the bear in the sailor suit to the window or light box. Transfer this design to the four remaining blocks of Doctor's flannel in the same manner as before.

Embroidery

Bear in striped top

Using the lightest shade of brown, outline the hands, body, legs, feet, head and ears with split stitch.

Striped top

Beginning at the lower edge and working upwards, embroider the body of the top in blue and white stripes. Stitch four rows of stem stitch close together for each stripe. Work the sleeves in the same manner.

Hands, body and legs

Fill the hands with long and short stitch. Embroider the body from the lower edge upwards. Begin with the darkest thread and grade to the lightest thread approximately one third of the way up.

Work the outer section of each foot with satin stitch and then the paw pad in the middle with long and short stitch. Outline the paw pad with a line

of stem stitch. Embroider the legs in the same manner as the hands.

Head

Work a fly stitch as the framework for the nose. Stitch the nose with satin stitch, covering the fly stitch, and then embroider a granitos for each eye. Working from the nose outwards, fill the muzzle with long and short stitches that radiate from the nose. Stitching from the muzzle outwards and grading from the darkest thread to the lightest, fill the remainder of the head with long and short stitch.

Using the darker shade for the inner ears, work each ear with long and short stitch.

Beret

Embroider closely worked rows of stem stitch across the top of the head for the beret. Fill the circle marked for the pompom with closely packed ghiordes knots. Comb and trim the knots until the threads are approximately 3mm (1/8") long.

Bear in sailor suit

Using the lightest shade of brown, outline the hands, body, legs, feet, head and ears with split stitch.

Jacket and tee-shirt

Beginning at the lower edge on one half of the collar, embroider four rows of stem stitch close together in the blanc thread. Change to the darker blue thread and work a single row of stem stitch in the same manner. Change back to the blanc thread and complete the collar with closely worked rows of stem stitch. Embroider the remaining half in exactly the same manner.

Add the knot at the centre of the collar with padded satin stitch and the ties with long and short stitch. Work the striped tee-shirt next, stitching each stripe with four rows of closely worked stem stitch.

Stitch the body of the jacket, and then the sleeves, with long and short stitch.

Hands, body, legs and head

Work these in exactly the same manner as the bear in the striped top.

Hat

Embroider closely worked rows of stem stitch across the top of the head for the band. Using the red thread, work the left hand side of the ribbon with vertical satin stitches and the right hand side with long and short stitch. Change to the light blue thread and work the remainder of the hat with vertical satin stitches as well.

Did you know?

Appleton crewel wool is the oldest and most popular crewel wool in the world. Having 421 hues and being loosely-twisted, shading techniques for Jacobean-style crewel embroidery are best achieved using Appleton Crewels.

Preparation for Quilting

Place each block face down on a well padded surface and press.

Sashing

Lay out the blocks, three per row, alternating between the two designs. Using a machine straight stitch, join the blocks following the instructions on page 120.

Borders

Stitch together the inner and outer border pieces for each side and end. Press. Attach the borders to the centrepiece following the instructions on pages 122 - 123. Press all pieces.

Layering

Spread the batting out flat and mark the centre of each side. With the right side to the inside, fold the quilt top into quarters. Position and baste it to the batting following the instructions on pages 125 - 127.

Quilting

Quilting the bears

Hand quilt around the outer edge of each bear so they stand out from the surrounding fabric.

Adding the lining

With the wrong side uppermost, spread the lining out flat. Layer and baste the padded quilt top to the lining in the same manner as the quilt top was attached to the batting.

Quilting the sashing and border

Hand quilt along the seamlines on each side of the horizontal pieces of sashing. Repeat along the edges of the vertical pieces of sashing, continuing across the horizontal pieces to mimic cornerstones *(diag 1)*.

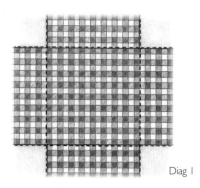

Diag 1

Repeat the procedure along both edges of the entire inner border.

Did you know?

Doctor's flannel is a fine, lightweight 100% wool, ideal for baby wraps.

EMBROIDERY KEY

All embroidery is worked with one strand unless otherwise specified.

Bear in striped top

Outlines = G (split stitch)

Hands = G (long and short stitch)

Body = D, E and G (long and short stitch)

Feet

Outer sections of feet = G (satin stitch)

Paw pads = D (long and short stitch)

Paw pad outlines = E (stem stitch)

Legs = G (long and short stitch)

Head

Nose = F (fly stitch, satin stitch)

Eyes = F (granitos)

Mouth = F (back stitch)

Muzzle = H (long and short stitch)

Face = D, E and G (long and short stitch)

Ears = E and G (long and short stitch)

Striped top = I and K (stem stitch)

Beret = K (stem stitch)

Pompom = J (ghiordes knot)

Bear in sailor suit

Outlines = G (split stitch)

Hands = G (long and short stitch)

Body = D, E and G (long and short stitch)

Feet

Outer sections of feet = G (satin stitch)

Paw pads = D (long and short stitch)

Paw pad outlines = E (stem stitch)

Legs = G (long and short stitch)

Head

Nose = F (fly stitch, satin stitch)

Eyes = F (granitos)

Mouth = F (back stitch)

Muzzle = H (long and short stitch)

Face = D, E and G (long and short stitch)

Ears = E and G (long and short stitch)

Jacket

Collar = I (stem stitch)

Collar stripe = K (stem stitch)

Body and sleeves = L (long and short stitch)

Knot = K (padded satin stitch)

Ties = K (long and short stitch)

Tee-shirt = I and K (stem stitch)

Hat

Band = K (stem stitch)

Crown = L (satin stitch)

Ribbon = J (satin stitch, long and short stitch)

Construction

*All seam allowances are 1cm (³/₈")
unless otherwise specified.*

1. Blocking

Block and square the quilt following
the instructions on page 135.

2. Attaching the piping

Cut two lengths of piping, each the
same length as the sides of the quilt
top. Aligning the piping stitchline
with the line between two rows of
checks, pin a length of piping to the
quilt top along each side. Stitch along
the piping stitchline *(diag 2).*

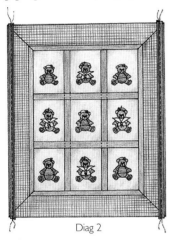

Diag 2

Cut two lengths of piping, each the
same length as the width of the quilt
top. Overlapping the previous pieces
of piping, pin and stitch a length to
each end of the quilt top in the same
manner as before.

3. Attaching the binding

Join the strips of binding together to
make one long length. Press the seams
open *(diag 3).* Fold the binding in half
along the length and press.

Diag 3

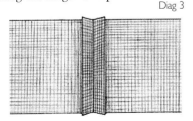

Beginning near the middle on one
side, attach the binding following the
instructions on pages 138 - 139.
Machine stitch just inside the previous
line of stitching along the piping.

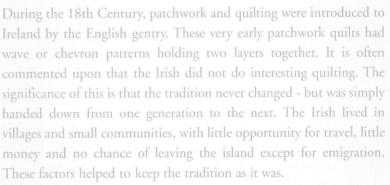

Why not stitch a bear onto a square of flannel and make a cushion
to match this charming quilt?

Irish Quilting

During the 18th Century, patchwork and quilting were introduced to
Ireland by the English gentry. These very early patchwork quilts had
wave or chevron patterns holding two layers together. It is often
commented upon that the Irish did not do interesting quilting. The
significance of this is that the tradition never changed - but was simply
handed down from one generation to the next. The Irish lived in
villages and small communities, with little opportunity for travel, little
money and no chance of leaving the island except for emigration.
These factors helped to keep the tradition as it was.

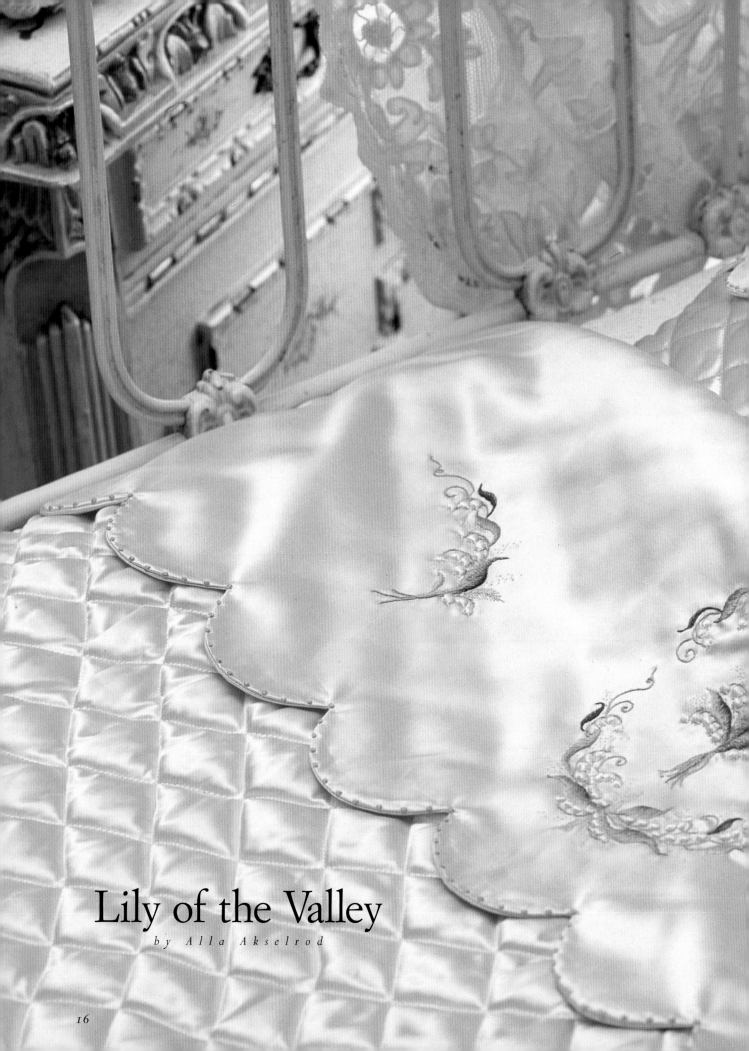

Lily of the Valley
by Alla Akselrod

Sized here for a cot, this magnificent design would also be superb for a larger bed.

Exquisite embroidery and lustrous satin

combine to create this luxurious set of quilt and pillowslip. Delicate sprays
of lily of the valley in soft fern greens and white adorn the gently scalloped edges.
Lines of diagonal quilting enhance the gleaming surface of the fabric
by creating an intriguing play of light and colour.

STITCHES AND TECHNIQUES

Fishbone stitch, Fly stitch
French knot, Granitos
Long and short stitch
Padded satin stitch
Satin stitch, Seed stitch
Stem stitch, Straight stitch
Whipped stem stitch
Straight machine quilting

Did you know?

In early times rattles, often
made of terracotta, were also
protective objects, thought to
drive away evil spirits.

Requirements

Fabric

Dusky green princess satin 3.5m x 112cm wide (3yd 29 3/4" x 44")

White polyester cotton batiste 1.4m x 112cm wide (1yd 19" x 44")

Embroidery threads

DMC stranded cotton

A = blanc

B = 520 dark fern green

C = 522 fern green

D = 523 light fern green

E = 524 very light fern green

F = 644 medium beige-grey

DMC stranded rayon

G = 35200 white

H = 30712 soft beige

Rajmahal artificial silk

I = 44 Tangier sand

Presencia stranded metallic thread

J = 9000 light gold

Supplies

Polyester wadding 1.2m x 140cm wide (1yd 12" x 55")

White lightweight non-woven interfacing 70cm x 90cm wide (27 1/2" x 35 1/2")

Pillow insert 29cm x 45cm wide (11 3/8" x 17 3/4")

Matching machine sewing thread

Fine water-soluble fabric marker

Tracing paper

Sharp HB pencil

Fine black pen

No. 10 crewel needle

The quilt measures 96cm x 77cm wide (37 ¾" x 30 ¼").

Cutting Out

See the liftout pattern sheet for the cutting layouts and templates.

Quilt

Quilt top: cut one from the satin, 91cm x 110cm wide (36" x 43 1/2")

Padding: cut one from the wadding, 110cm x 91cm wide (43 1/2" x 36")

Upper scalloped border: cut two from the princess satin and one from the interfacing, each 80cm x 30cm wide (31 1/2" x 11 3/4")

Lower scalloped border: cut two from the princess satin and one from the interfacing, each 80cm x 16cm wide (31 1/2" x 6 1/4")

Interlining: cut one from the batiste, 91cm x 110cm wide (36" x 43 1/2")

Pillowslip

Pillowslip front: cut one from the princess satin, 56cm x 40cm wide (22" x 15 3/4")

Padding: cut one from the wadding, 56cm x 40cm wide (22" x 15 3/4")

Scalloped border: cut two from the princess satin and one from the interfacing, each 48cm x 18cm wide (19" x 7")

Lining: cut one from the batiste, 48cm x 32cm wide (19" x 12 5/8")

Cut out all other pieces following the instructions on the liftout pattern sheet.

Preparation for Embroidery

Transferring the designs

See the liftout pattern sheet for the embroidery designs.

Using the black pen, trace the embroidery designs, scallops and placement marks for the upper border of the quilt onto tracing paper. Tape the tracing to a window or light box. With the right side of one upper border piece facing you, centre it over the tracing. Align the lower edge of the fabric with the placement marks. Tape in place. Using the pencil, trace the stems and outlines for the flowers and leaves. The scallops will be transferred after the main embroidery is complete.

Transfer the embroidery designs to one border piece for the pillowslip in the same manner.

Embroidery

Quilt

Central spray

Embroider the large middle leaf first. Shading from dark to light, fill the leaf with long and short stitch, working 2 - 3 layers to give a raised effect. Stitch the remaining two leaves in the same manner.

Work all the stems, using either stem stitch or whipped stem stitch. Add the tiny satin stitch leaves.

Embroider the lily of the valley flowers next. Build up each flower by working several layers of satin stitch, ensuring each layer lies in the opposite direction to the previous layer. For the final layer, use the same hole at the base of the flower for every stitch. Work two French knots below each flower for stamens.

Stitch the sprays of gypsophila with a mix of seed stitches and French knots.

Garland

Work the leaves, stems and flowers in the same manner as the spray. Add the tendrils with stem stitch. Work three fern fronds near the centre of each section. Begin each of the larger fronds with a fly stitch at the tip, then work the remainder with fishbone stitch. Embroider the smallest frond with satin stitch.

Side sprays

Embroider the sprays on each side of the central design in the same manner as the garland.

Dots on scallops

Add the dots along the scalloped edges of both the upper and lower borders after the scallops have been formed. Each dot is a granitos of 8 - 10 stitches.

Pillowslip

Large spray

Stitch this spray in the same manner as the central spray on the quilt, adding a fern frond on each side at the base of the flowers. Work the bow with satin stitch and add the straight stitch highlights with the metallic thread.

Small sprays

Embroider these in a similar manner to the large spray.

Dots on scallops

Add the dots along the scalloped edge after the scallops have been formed. Each dot is a granitos of 8 - 10 stitches.

> ## Did you know?
>
> "An old-time quilt maker used a needle as often, as easily, as casually as we use a telephone: it was her duty, her comfort, her companion, her mode of self-expression."

Preparation for Quilting

Quilt

Spread the white batiste interlining out flat and mark the centre of each side. Position and baste the wadding and quilt top to the interlining following the instructions on pages 125 - 127.

Rule a diagonal line across the centre of the quilt top with the fabric marker.

Pillowslip

Prepare the pillowslip front in exactly the same manner as the quilt.

Quilting

Quilt

Work a row of machine straight stitch along the marked line. Turn the quilt around and work a parallel line 3.5cm (1 1/2") away from the first line. Continue in this manner until the quilt is completely covered with parallel lines 3.5cm (1 1/2") apart.

Repeat the procedure in the opposite direction, forming diamonds.

Pillowslip

Quilt the pillowslip front in exactly the same manner.

Sashiko

The Japanese word sashiko means 'little stabs', or running stitch. The Japanese used this simple and practical technique to piece together several layers of loosely woven fabric for strength and warmth.

In the 15th century cotton was introduced to Japan, but earlier fabrics were made from grass, tree-bark fibres or silk.

EMBROIDERY KEY

All embroidery is worked with one strand unless otherwise specified.

Lily of the valley

Petals = A (2 strands, straight stitch), G (padded satin stitch, straight stitch)

Stamens = I
(French knot, 1 - 2 wraps)

Stems

Leaf stems = B and C
(stem stitch, whipped stem stitch)

Flower stems = D (stem stitch, whipped stem stitch)

Tendrils = D (stem stitch)

Leaves

Large leaves = B, C and D
(long and short stitch)

Medium leaves = B and C
(long and short stitch)

Small leaves = C and D
(long and short stitch)

Tiny leaves = F (satin stitch)

Fern fronds = F
(fly stitch, fishbone stitch)

Gypsophila = A
(seed stitch, French knot, 1 wrap)

Bow (on pillowslip)

Bow = H (satin stitch)

Highlights = J (straight stitch)

Dots on scallops = E (granitos)

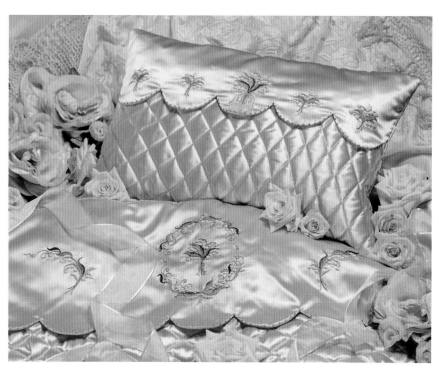

The pillowslip measures 29cm x 45cm wide (11 3/8" x 17 3/4").

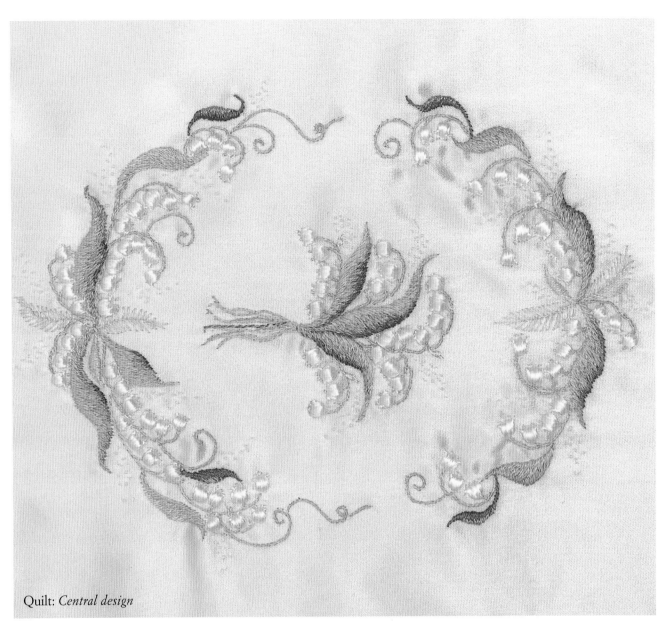

Quilt: *Central design*

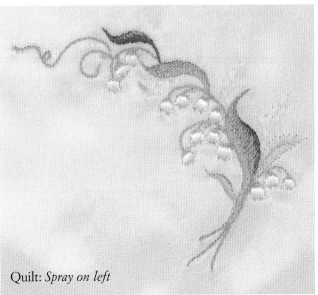

Quilt: *Spray on left*

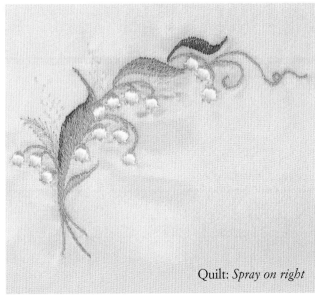

Quilt: *Spray on right*

Pillowslip: *Large spray*

Pillowslip: *Small spray*

Construction

All seam allowances are 1.5cm ($^5/8$") unless otherwise specified.

QUILT

1. Forming the upper scalloped border

Tape the upper border embroidery and scallop tracing to a window or light box. Centre the interfacing for the upper border over the tracing, aligning the lower edge of the interfacing with the placement marks on the tracing. Tape in place. Using the lead pencil, trace the stitchlines for the scallops.

Place the embroidered border and the backing piece right sides together. Place the interfacing onto the wrong side of the embroidered piece. Ensure the traced scallops are uppermost and are centred over the embroidery (*diag 1*).

Diag 1

Pin, tack and machine stitch along the marked stitchline, pivoting at the point of each scallop. Trim the seam allowance close to the stitching and clip the points (*diag 2*). Turn through to the right side and press.

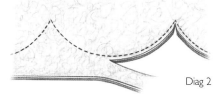

Diag 2

2. Forming the lower scalloped border

Form the scallops on the lower border in the same manner as the upper border.

3. Embroidering the dots

Mark and embroider the raised dots along the scalloped edges following the instructions on page 21.

4. Squaring the quilt top

Square the quilt following the instructions on page 135.

5. Attaching the borders

Lay the quilt out flat with the right side uppermost. With raw edges even and the embroidered side uppermost, place the upper border onto one end of the quilt. Pin and tack the layers together around the straight outer edges (*diag 3*).

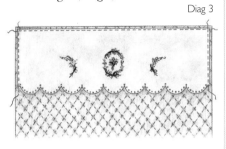

Diag 3

Repeat at the opposite end with the lower border.

6. Attaching the lining

With right sides together and raw edges even, pin and tack the lining to the quilt. The borders are sandwiched between. Stitch, leaving a 30cm (12") opening in the middle of one long side (*diag 4*).

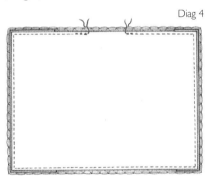

Diag 4

Turn the quilt through to the right side and carefully handstitch the opening closed.

PILLOWSLIP

1. Forming the upper scalloped border

Form the scalloped border and embroider the raised dots following the instructions in steps 1 and 3 for the quilt.

2. Squaring the pillowslip front

Square the pillowslip front following the instructions on page 135.

3. Attaching the border

Attach the border following step 5 for the quilt.

4. Forming the back

Neaten one long side of each back piece, with a 6mm (1/4") machine stitched double hem. With right sides together and raw edges even along the sides, pin the two pieces together so the upper piece is 8cm (3 1/8") away from the bottom edge of the lower piece.

Leaving a 19cm (7 1/2") opening in the middle, stitch along the neatened side using a 2.5cm (1") seam allowance (*diag 5*).

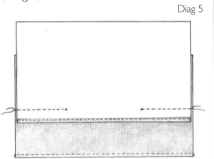

Diag 5

Press the seam allowance and extending fabric to one side (*diag 6*).

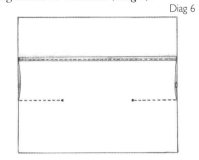

Diag 6

Tack the layers together along the short sides.

5. Attaching the back

With right sides together and raw edges even, pin and tack the front to the back. The border is sandwiched between. Stitch around all sides (*diag 7*). Turn to the right side through the opening in the centre back.

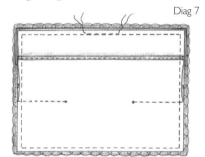

Diag 7

The Lily of the Valley

- This flower is also known as Our Lady's tears. Other names include May Lily, May Bells, Lily Constancy, Ladder-to-Heaven, Male Lily and Muguet.

- According to legend, the tears Mary shed at the cross turned to Lilies of the Valley.

- By tradition, Lily of the Valley is sold in France in the streets on May 1st.

- In 1982, Lily of the Valley became the national flower of Finland.

THE LILY OF THE VALE, OF FLOWERS THE QUEEN,
PUTS ON THE ROBE SHE NEITHER SEW'D NOR SPUN.

MICHEAL BRUCE, ELEGY

For the love
of Butterflies

Vibrant fabrics and exotic butterflies vie for attention

on this magnificent queen bed quilt. Twenty blocks of sixteen squares form the central panel, each block embroidered with one or two glorious insects in glowing silk. A double band of rust borders a strip of tiny jewel like squares that surround the centre. The quilt is backed with floral print cotton and bound with rust.

STITCHES AND TECHNIQUES

Back stitch, Blanket stitch
Fly stitch, French knot
Long and short stitch
Padded satin stitch
Satin stitch, Seed stitch
Split stitch, Straight stitch
Piecing by machine
Freeform machine quilting

Requirements

Fabric

A = rust *Liberty* Tana lawn
1.2m x 137cm wide (1yd 11 1/4" x 54")

B = red floral print cotton
5.4m x 112cm wide (5yd 33" x 44")

488 x 11.2cm (4 1/2") squares
Liberty print fabric

616 x 4cm (1 1/2") squares
Liberty print fabric

8 x 13cm (5") squares
Liberty print fabric

8 x 6.5cm (2 1/2") squares
Liberty print fabric

Embroidery threads and needle

See pages 31 - 45.

Supplies

Cotton batting 2.8m x 230cm wide
(3yd 2 1/4" x 130")

Ecru machine quilting thread

Tracing paper

Sharp lead pencil

Fine black pen

Embroidery hoop 15cm (6") wide

Cutting Out

Use 320 of the 11.2cm (4 1/2") *Liberty* print patches for the embroidered blocks.

Cut any other pieces following the instructions on the liftout pattern sheet.

Did you know?

The oldest surviving example of patchwork is a quilted Egyptian canopy used by the Queen for festive occasions in 980 BC. It now resides in the Egyptian Museum in Cairo.

Preparation for Embroidery

Transferring the designs

See the liftout pattern sheet for the embroidery designs.

Using a 6mm (1/4") seam allowance, piece together sixteen patches of fabric to form a square block. Repeat this process nineteen more times. Carefully press each one.

Using the fine black pen, trace each embroidery design onto a separate piece of tracing paper. Tape one tracing

Embroidered by Susan O'Connor and quilted by Lyn Hughes

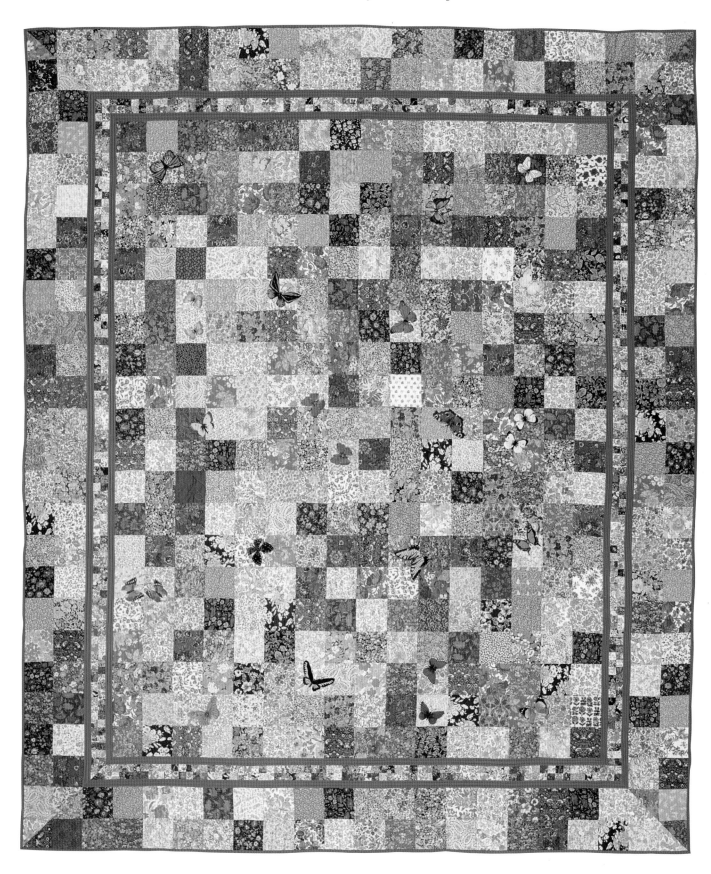

The quilt measures 263cm x 222cm wide (142 1/2" x 126 5/8").

to a window or light box. With the right side of a block facing you, place it over the tracing, ensuring the design is positioned and orientated the way you wish. Tape in place. Using the lead pencil, trace the design onto the fabric. Repeat the procedure for the remaining nineteen embroidery designs.

Embroidery

1. VICEROY BUTTERFLY

All embroidery is worked with the no. 10 sharp needle. Use the photograph as a guide to thread colour changes within the design.

Wings

Outline all four wings with split stitch. Fill the upper wings with long and short stitch. Using the same thread colour, begin working the lower wings near the outer edges. Change to the light mahogany thread and then the light tangerine thread as you work towards the butterfly's body. Stitch the edges with satin stitch and then the veins with long and short stitch. Add the white spots with either satin stitch or several straight stitches close together.

Body

Outline the body in the same manner as the wings. Fill the body with stitches that run along the length for padding. Cover the padding with satin stitches that lay across the body. Add two tiny seed stitches for the eyes. Stitch the antennae with back stitch and finish with several straight stitches close together for the clubbed ends.

THREADS AND NEEDLE FOR VICEROY BUTTERFLY

Madeira stranded silk

A = 0113 light tangerine
B = 2306 mahogany
C = 2307 light mahogany
D = 2400 black
E = 2401 white
No. 10 sharp needle

EMBROIDERY KEY FOR VICEROY BUTTERFLY

All embroidery is worked with one strand unless otherwise specified.

Wings

Outlines = D (split stitch)

Upper wings = B (long and short stitch, satin stitch), D (satin stitch)

Lower wings = A, B and C (long and short stitch), D (satin stitch)

Veins = D (long and short stitch)

Spots = E
(satin stitch, straight stitch)

Body

Outlines = D (split stitch)

Body = D (padded satin stitch)

Eyes = E (seed stitch)

Antennae = D
(back stitch, straight stitch)

2. PAIR OF ORANGE SULPHUR BUTTERFLIES

All embroidery is worked with the no. 10 sharp needle. Use the photograph as a guide to thread colour changes within the design. Both butterflies are embroidered in exactly the same manner.

Wings

Outline all four wings with split stitch. Fill the wings with long and short stitch and then add the veins over the top of the previous stitching. Embroider the spots with satin stitch. After the wings are embroidered, work a split stitch outline around each one for definition.

Body

Outline the body with split stitch. Working across the body, fill both the abdomen and thorax with satin stitch. Add tiny satin stitches along the edges with the black-brown thread and then several back stitches around the lower end. Using the same thread colour as the thorax, embroider the stripes on the abdomen and then the eyes and antennae. Stitch several straight stitches close together for the clubbed ends of the antennae.

THREADS AND NEEDLE FOR PAIR OF ORANGE SULPHUR BUTTERFLIES

Madeira stranded silk

A = 0105 canary yellow
B = 0112 light primrose
C = 0113 light tangerine
D = 2004 black-brown
E = 2008 brown
F = 2114 medium hazelnut brown
No. 10 sharp needle

EMBROIDERY KEY FOR PAIR OF ORANGE SULPHUR BUTTERFLIES

All embroidery is worked with one strand unless otherwise specified.

Wings

Outlines = A and B (split stitch)

Upper wings = A, C, D, E and F (long and short stitch)

Spots on upper wings = D (satin stitch)

Lower wings = A, B and E (long and short stitch)

Spots on lower wings = C (satin stitch)

Veins = F (split stitch)

Body

Outlines = D (split stitch, back stitch)

Thorax = E (satin stitch)

Abdomen = B and D (satin stitch)

Stripes on abdomen = E (straight stitch)

Eyes = E (French knot, 2 wraps)

Antennae = E (back stitch, straight stitch)

Did you know?

The first sewing needles were hand-made out of bone, over 17,000 years ago by western Europeans and central Asians.

3. COPPER BUTTERFLY

All embroidery is worked with the no. 10 sharp needle. Use the photograph as a guide to thread colour changes within the design.

Wings

Outline all four wings with split stitch. Fill the upper wings with long and short stitch, working the brown patches with satin stitch. Embroider the edges and spots on the lower wings with satin stitch. Fill in the remainder of these wings with long and short stitch and a small amount of satin stitch. Add the yellow veins on both the upper and lower wings with straight stitch, working the long lines on the upper wings with split stitch.

Body

Outline the head and thorax in the same manner as the wings. Fill these with satin stitch, leaving a space for the marking on the thorax. Using the canary yellow thread, embroider the marking and each section of the abdomen. Change to the green thread and work the split stitch stripes across the abdomen. Add a single straight stitch to the marking on the thorax and several straight stitches to the tip of the abdomen. Embroider two tiny seed stitches for the eyes. Stitch the antennae with back stitch and finish with several straight stitches close together for the clubbed ends. Finally, stitch the partial outlines on the head and around the thorax.

THREADS AND NEEDLE FOR COPPER BUTTERFLY

Madeira stranded silk

A = 0105 canary yellow
B = 0112 light primrose
C = 0113 light tangerine
D = 0401 dark terracotta
E = 0402 medium terracotta
F = 1408 avocado green
G = 2004 black-brown
H = 2006 dark brown
No. 10 sharp needle

EMBROIDERY KEY FOR COPPER BUTTERFLY

All embroidery is worked with one strand unless otherwise specified.

Wings

Outlines = G (split stitch)

Upper wings = D, E and G (long and short stitch, satin stitch), H (satin stitch)

Lower wings = D (long and short stitch, split stitch), E (long and short stitch), C (long and short stitch, satin stitch)

Edging on lower wings = G (satin stitch)

Veins = C (straight stitch, split stitch)

Spots on lower wings = G (satin stitch)

Body

Outlines = G (split stitch)

Head = G (satin stitch)

Thorax = G (satin stitch)

Marking on thorax = A (satin stitch), F (straight stitch)

Abdomen = A (satin stitch)

Stripes on abdomen = F (split stitch, straight stitch)

Eyes = B (seed stitch)

Antennae = G (back stitch, straight stitch)

Partial outlines on head and thorax = H (back stitch)

4. BLACK VEINED WHITE BUTTERFLY

All embroidery is worked with the no. 10 sharp needle. Use the photograph as a guide to thread colour changes within the design.

Wings

Outline all four wings with split stitch and fill with long and short stitch. Work around the edge of each wing with split stitch, then use long split stitches to form the veins.

Body

Outline the body in the same manner as the wings. Fill the body with stitches that run along the length for padding. Cover the padding with satin stitches that lay across the body. Using satin and straight stitches, work the black markings over the previous stitching. Finish the abdomen with a fly stitch at the lower end. Embroider the head with satin stitch and add two tiny seed stitches for the eyes. Stitch the antennae with back stitch and several straight stitches close together for the clubbed ends. Finish each one with a tiny fly stitch around the tip.

THREADS AND NEEDLE FOR BLACK VEINED WHITE BUTTERFLY

Madeira stranded silk

A = 1803 light grey
B = 1912 mocha
C = 2004 black-brown
D = 2400 black
E = 2401 white
No. 10 sharp needle

EMBROIDERY KEY FOR BLACK VEINED WHITE BUTTERFLY

All embroidery is worked with one strand unless otherwise specified.

Wings

Outlines = E (split stitch)

Upper wings = B and E (long and short stitch)

Lower wings = B, C and E (long and short stitch)

Veins = C (split stitch)

Edging = C (split stitch)

Body

Outlines = A and D (split stitch)

Body = A (padded satin stitch)

Body markings = D (satin stitch, straight stitch, fly stitch)

Head = D (padded satin stitch)

Eyes = E (seed stitch)

Antennae = D (back stitch, straight stitch), E (fly stitch)

5. PAIR OF COMMON GRASS-BLUE BUTTERFLIES

All embroidery is worked with the no. 10 sharp needle. Use the photograph as a guide to thread colour changes within the design. Both butterflies are embroidered in exactly the same manner.

Wings

Outline all wings with split stitch. Covering the outlines, fill each wing with long and short stitch. Using the blue-grey thread, outline each wing with back stitch and then work the wing markings with straight stitch. Add the veins to the lower wings with long split stitches. Embroider several straight stitches over the upper wings with the tan thread.

Body

Outline the body in the same manner as the wings. Fill the body and head with vertical satin stitches. Add straight stitches across the thorax and abdomen for markings. Space the stitches further apart on the abdomen than on the thorax. Finish the abdomen with a fly stitch around the tip. Stitch the eyes with satin stitch and the antennae with back stitch, adding several straight stitches close together for the clubbed ends.

THREADS AND NEEDLE FOR PAIR OF COMMON GRASS-BLUE BUTTERFLIES

Madeira stranded silk

A = 0806 dark antique violet
B = 0807 light antique violet
C = 1712 dark blue-grey
D = 2004 black-brown
E = 2012 tan
No. 10 sharp needle

The butterfly is a flying flower,
The flower a tethered butterfly.

ECOUCHARD LE BRUN

EMBROIDERY KEY FOR PAIR OF COMMON GRASS-BLUE BUTTERFLIES

All embroidery is worked with one strand unless otherwise specified.

Wings

Outlines = A (split stitch),
C (back stitch)

Upper wings = A and B
(long and short stitch)

Markings on upper wings = C and E (straight stitch)

Lower wings = A and B
(long and short stitch)

Markings on lower wings = C
(straight stitch)

Veins on lower wings = C
(split stitch)

Body

Outlines = E (split stitch)

Thorax and head = C (satin stitch)

Abdomen = C and E (satin stitch)

Markings on body = D
(straight stitch)

Tip of abdomen = D (fly stitch)

Eyes = D (satin stitch)

Antennae = D
(back stitch, straight stitch)

6. CAIRNS BIRDWING

All embroidery is worked with the no. 10 sharp needle. Use the photograph as a guide to thread colour changes within the design.

Wings

Outline the wings with split stitch and fill with long and short stitch. On the upper wings, work straight stitches along the green stripes in the middle. Add the black spots to the lower wings with satin stitch.

Body

Outline the body in the same manner as the wings. Fill the body with stitches that run along the length for padding. Cover the padding with satin stitches that lie across the body, using the black thread for the head and thorax and the yellow thread for the abdomen. Add the green markings to the thorax with straight stitches, then the black markings to the abdomen in the same manner, working a tiny section of satin stitch at the tip.

Embroider seed stitches for the eyes and then change to the brown thread. Work a tiny straight stitch between the eyes, one at the base of the head and two on each side of the body. Stitch the antennae with back stitch and finish with several straight stitches close together for the clubbed ends.

THREADS AND NEEDLE FOR CAIRNS BIRDWING

Madeira stranded silk

A = 0105 canary yellow
B = 1405 dark hunter green
C = 1407 hunter green
D = 2008 brown
E = 2400 black
No. 10 sharp needle

EMBROIDERY KEY FOR CAIRNS BIRDWING

All embroidery is worked with one strand unless otherwise specified.

Wings

Outlines = E (split stitch)

Upper wings = C (long and short stitch), E (long and short stitch, straight stitch)

Lower wings = B, C and E
(long and short stitch)

Spots on lower wings = E
(satin stitch)

Body

Outlines = E (split stitch)

Head and thorax = E
(padded satin stitch)

Markings on head and abdomen
= D and C (straight stitch)

Abdomen = A (padded satin stitch)

Markings on abdomen = E
(straight stitch, satin stitch)

Eyes = C (seed stitch)

Antennae = E
(back stitch, straight stitch)

1. *Viceroy butterfly*

2. *Orange sulphur butterfly (pair)*

3. *Copper butterfly*

4. *Black veined white butterfly*

5. *Common grass-blue butterfly (pair)*

6. *Cairns birdwing*

7. *Cramer's blue morpho*

8. *Madagascar emigrant*

9. *Orange sulphur butterfly*

10. *African sangaris (pair)*

11. *Peacock butterfly*

12. *Cabbage butterfly (pair)*

13. *Spotted red butterfly (pair)*

14. *Queen cracker*

15. *Tiger swallowtail*

16. *Green swallowtail*

17. *Orange albatross*

18. *Rajah Brooke's birdwing*

19. *Adonis blue (pair)*

20. *Blomfild's beauty*

7. CRAMER'S BLUE MORPHO

All embroidery is worked with the no. 10 sharp needle. Use the photograph as a guide to thread colour changes within the design.

Wings

Using the peacock blue thread, outline all four wings with split stitch. Fill the upper wings with long and short stitch using the black and dark sky blue threads near the base and tip of each wing. Add each white spot with two straight stitches that form a narrow 'V' shape.

Embroider the middle of the lower wings in the same manner as the upper wings. Add a black and brown strip to the upper edge of each wing and a black, brown and tan strip to the lower edge. Stitch the veins with long split stitches.

Body

Outline the body in the same manner as the wings. Fill the body with stitches that run along the length for padding. Cover the padding with satin stitches that lie across the body. Embroider the antennae with back stitch and finish with several straight stitches close together for the clubbed ends.

THREADS AND NEEDLE FOR CRAMER'S BLUE MORPHO

Madeira stranded silk

A = 1005 dark sky blue
B = 1103 dark peacock blue
C = 2014 ultra light tan
D = 2114 medium hazelnut brown
E = 2400 black
F = 2401 white

No. 10 sharp needle

EMBROIDERY KEY FOR CRAMER'S BLUE MORPHO

All embroidery is worked with one strand unless otherwise specified.

Wings

Outlines = B (split stitch)

Upper wings = A, B and E (long and short stitch)

Lower wings = A, B, C, D and E (long and short stitch)

Veins = E (split stitch)

Spots on upper wings = F (straight stitch)

Body

Outlines = E (split stitch)

Body = E (padded satin stitch)

Antennae = E (back stitch, straight stitch)

8. MADAGASCAR EMIGRANT

All embroidery is worked with the no. 10 sharp needle. Use the photograph as a guide to thread colour changes within the design.

Wings

Outline the wings with split stitch. Beginning at the outer edge and working towards the body, fill each wing with long and short stitch. Add several blue-grey straight stitches along each side near the body. Stitch all the spots with satin stitch, working them over the previous stitching. Add the veins with long straight stitches and divide the wings with split stitch.

Body

Outline the body in the same manner as the wings. Using the light primrose thread, fill the body with stitches that run along the length for padding. Cover the padding with satin stitches that lie across the body, changing thread colour for each body segment. Add two pairs of fly stitches to the thorax and a single straight stitch to the head for markings. Stitch the antennae with split stitch and finish with several straight stitches close together for the clubbed ends.

THREADS AND NEEDLE FOR MADAGASCAR EMIGRANT

Madeira stranded silk

A = 0105 canary yellow
B = 0112 light primrose
C = 0113 light tangerine
D = 0306 light apricot
E = 1710 light blue-grey
F = 1914 coffee brown
G = 2211 topaz
H = 2401 white
I = 2404 ecru

No. 10 sharp needle

EMBROIDERY KEY FOR MADAGASCAR EMIGRANT

All embroidery is worked with one strand unless otherwise specified.

Wings

Outlines = A (split stitch)

Upper wings = A, B, D and H (long and short stitch), E (straight stitch)

Light spots on upper wings = G (satin stitch)

Dark spots on upper wings = F (satin stitch)

Lower wings = A, B, D and H (long and short stitch), E (straight stitch)

Spots on lower wings = C (satin stitch)

Veins = A (straight stitch)

Division between wings = C (split stitch)

Body

Outlines = D (split stitch)

Head = B (padded satin stitch)

Marking on head = D (straight stitch)

Thorax = D (padded satin stitch)

Markings on thorax = E (fly stitch)

Abdomen = B (padded satin stitch)

Antennae = I (split stitch, straight stitch)

9. ORANGE SULPHUR BUTTERFLY

All embroidery is worked with the no. 10 sharp needle. Use the photograph as a guide to thread colour changes within the design.

Wings

Outline all four wings with split stitch. Fill the upper wings with long and short stitch. Work coffee brown satin stitch stripes over the brown sections.

Using the same thread colour, begin working the lower wings near the outer edges. Work towards the butterfly's body with long and short stitch. Add the yellow veins to both pairs of wings and then work straight stitches of varying lengths near the body. Use both the orange and black threads on the upper wings and the black thread only on the lower wings. Embroider a satin stitch spot on each wing, using the coffee brown thread for the upper wings and the orange thread for the lower wings.

Body

Outline the body with split stitch. Pad the thorax with stitches that lie across the body and then cover with stitches that lie along the length. Add two black fly stitches near the top and a patch of black satin stitch near the lower end for markings. Embroider the abdomen with padded satin stitch, ensuring the padding stitches run along the length and the satin stitches lie across the abdomen.

Using the same thread colour, stitch two satin stitch spots for the eyes. Add a seed stitch to the centre of each spot. Embroider the antennae with back stitch and then work several straight stitches close together for the clubbed ends.

THREADS AND NEEDLE FOR ORANGE SULPHUR BUTTERFLY

Madeira stranded silk

A = 0103 light canary yellow
B = 0105 canary yellow
C = 0113 light tangerine
D = 0204 orange
E = 1914 coffee brown
F = 2008 brown
G = 2400 black
No. 10 sharp needle

EMBROIDERY KEY FOR ORANGE SULPHUR BUTTERFLY

All embroidery is worked with one strand unless otherwise specified.

Wings

Upper wing outlines = C and F (split stitch)

Lower wing outlines = B and E (split stitch)

Upper wings = C and F (long and short stitch), E (satin stitch), D and G (straight stitch)

Spots on upper wings = E (satin stitch)

Lower wings = A, B, C and E (long and short stitch), G (straight stitch)

Spots on lower wings = D (satin stitch)

Veins = B (split stitch)

Body

Outlines = G (split stitch)

Thorax = E (padded satin stitch)

Markings on thorax = G (fly stitch, satin stitch)

Abdomen = G (padded satin stitch)

Eyes = G (satin stitch), B (seed stitch)

Antennae = G (back stitch, straight stitch)

> "There is no antique more expressive of our foremothers than patchwork, which, in the main, took the form of bed-quilts. Pieced or appliquéd, the quilt has been, in America, a wholly feminine creation." *Ruth E. Finley (1929)*

10. PAIR OF AFRICAN SANGARIS

All embroidery is worked with the no. 10 sharp needle. Use the photograph as a guide to thread colour changes within the design. Both butterflies are embroidered in exactly the same manner.

Wings

Using the orange-red thread, outline the upper wings with split stitch and fill with long and short stitch. Repeat for the lower wings, using the gold and brown threads near the body. Add the veins to both pairs of wings, using a combination of fly and split stitches. Change to the black-brown thread and work several straight stitches on each wing near the body. Add the spots to the lower wings and the tips to the upper wings with the same thread.

Body

Outline the body in the same manner as the wings. Fill the body with stitches that run along the length for padding. Cover the padding with satin stitches that lie across the body.

Add two tiny seed stitches for the eyes. Using the black-brown thread, stitch the markings on the thorax and abdomen, and define the eyes. Change to the gold thread and complete the body markings with a fly stitch and two straight stitches. Partially outline the body with a single row of back stitches. Embroider the antennae with split stitch and finish with several straight stitches close together for the clubbed ends.

THREADS AND NEEDLE FOR PAIR OF AFRICAN SANGARIS

Madeira stranded silk

A = 0210 bright orange-red
B = 0812 shell pink
C = 2004 black-brown
D = 2008 brown
E = 2210 dark old gold
No. 10 sharp needle

EMBROIDERY KEY FOR PAIR OF AFRICAN SANGARIS

All embroidery is worked with one strand unless otherwise specified.

Wings

Outlines = A (split stitch), C (back stitch)

Upper wings = A (long and short stitch), C (straight stitch)

Lower wings = A, B and D (long and short stitch), C and E (straight stitch)

Veins = B (fly stitch, split stitch)

Spots = C (satin stitch, straight stitch)

Body

Outlines = D (split stitch)

Body = D (padded satin stitch)

Markings = C (fly stitch, satin stitch, straight stitch), E (fly stitch, straight stitch, split stitch)

Eyes = E (seed stitch)

Antennae = C (split stitch, straight stitch)

11. PEACOCK BUTTERFLY

All embroidery is worked with the no. 10 sharp needle. Use the photograph as a guide to thread colour changes within the design.

Wings

Outline all four wings with split stitch. Fill each upper wing with long and short stitch, leaving a space for the large spot. Near the body, work straight stitches of varying lengths. Stitch the large spots next and then work the small spots over the previous stitching. Add the veins with long split stitches and the black markings to the front of the wings with straight stitches.

Embroider the lower wings from the outer edges towards the body, leaving spaces for the spots. On each wing, add a fan of straight stitches near the body and then embroider the spot.

Body

Outline the body in the same manner as the wings. Embroider the head with padded satin stitch and then the thorax with long and short stitch. Add the straight stitch markings. To create the abdomen, work a series of straight stitches across the body and then work several short straight stitches in the opposite direction.

Embroider the French knot eyes and the markings on the head. Stitch the antennae with split stitch, finishing with several straight stitches close together for the clubbed ends.

THREADS AND NEEDLE FOR PEACOCK BUTTERFLY

Madeira stranded silk

A = 0105 canary yellow
B = 0402 medium terracotta
C = 0511 medium garnet
D = 0806 dark antique violet
E = 0811 dark shell pink
F = 1005 dark sky blue
G = 1912 mocha
H = 1914 coffee brown
I = 2004 black-brown
J = 2008 brown
K = 2400 black
L = 2401 white

No. 10 sharp needle

EMBROIDERY KEY FOR PEACOCK BUTTERFLY

All embroidery is worked with one strand unless otherwise specified.

Wings

Outlines = I (split stitch)

Upper wings = A, E and I (long and short stitch), K (satin stitch), I and J (straight stitch)

Large spots on upper wings = A, D and I (long and short stitch), E, F and L (straight stitch)

Small spots on upper wings = D, F and L (straight stitch)

Markings on front of upper wings = K (straight stitch)

Lower wings = E and I (long and short stitch), J (long and short stitch, straight stitch)

Spots on lower wings = F, G, K and L (long and short stitch)

Veins on upper wings = C (split stitch)

Body

Outlines = H and J (split stitch)

Thorax = H (long and short stitch), B and G (straight stitch)

Abdomen = G, I and J (straight stitch)

Head = H (padded satin stitch)

Markings on head = K (straight stitch, fly stitch)

Eyes = H (French knot, 2 wraps)

Antennae = K (split stitch, straight stitch)

12. PAIR OF CABBAGE BUTTERFLIES

All embroidery is worked with the no. 10 sharp needle. Use the photograph as a guide to thread colour changes within the design. Both butterflies are stitched in exactly the same manner.

Wings

Outline all four wings with split stitch and fill with long and short stitch. Using the black and grey threads, work straight stitches of varying lengths on the inner wings. Add a black satin stitch spot to each upper wing, stitching over the previous embroidery. Work the veins with very long split stitches.

Body

Outline the body in the same manner as the wings. Fill the body with stitches that run along the length for padding. Cover the padding with satin stitches that lie across the body. Stitch the antennae with back stitch and finish with several straight stitches close together for the clubbed ends.

THREADS AND NEEDLE FOR PAIR OF CABBAGE BUTTERFLIES

Madeira stranded silk

A = 1710 light blue-grey
B = 2013 very light tan
C = 2400 black
D = 2401 white
No. 10 sharp needle

EMBROIDERY KEY FOR PAIR OF CABBAGE BUTTERFLIES

All embroidery is worked with one strand unless otherwise specified.

Wings

Outlines = C and D (split stitch)

Upper wings = D (long and short stitch), C (long and short stitch, straight stitch), A (straight stitch)

Spots on upper wings = C (satin stitch)

Lower wings = D (long and short stitch), C (long and short stitch, straight stitch), A (straight stitch)

Veins = B (split stitch)

Body

Outlines = C (split stitch)

Body = C (padded satin stitch)

Antennae = C (back stitch, straight stitch)

13. PAIR OF SPOTTED RED BUTTERFLIES

All embroidery is worked with the no. 10 sharp needle. Use the photograph as a guide to thread colour changes within the design. Both butterflies are embroidered in a similar manner.

Wings

Outline all four wings with split stitch. Beginning near the outer edge, embroider the upper wings with long and short stitch, leaving spaces for the violet spots. Stitch the spots with satin stitch.

Work the outer sections of the lower wings with satin stitch and then change to long and short stitch for the remainder. Use the brown and the dark terracotta threads for the outer sections of the lower wings on the left hand butterfly. Use the brown and the dark shell pink threads for the outer sections of the lower wings on the right hand butterfly.

Embroider the veins next, using straight stitches and long split stitches.

Define the lower edges of the upper wings with two rows of split stitch, one dark brown and one violet. Finally, embroider two split stitch stripes on each lower wing.

Body

Outline the body in the same manner as the wings. Fill each segment of the body with satin stitch and then work the straight stitch markings. Stitch the divisions on the abdomen and the thorax outline with split stitch.

Work two padded satin stitch spots close together and add two tiny seed stitches for the eyes. Stitch the antennae with back stitch and finish with several straight stitches close together for the clubbed ends.

THREADS AND NEEDLE FOR PAIR OF SPOTTED RED BUTTERFLIES

Madeira stranded silk

A = 0105 canary yellow
B = 0401 dark terracotta
C = 0402 medium terracotta
D = 0711 medium violet
E = 0811 dark shell pink
F = 2004 black-brown
G = 2006 dark brown
H = 2401 white
No. 10 sharp needle

EMBROIDERY KEY FOR PAIR OF SPOTTED RED BUTTERFLIES

All embroidery is worked with one strand unless otherwise specified.

Wings

Outlines = C and F (split stitch)

Upper wings = B, C, E and F (long and short stitch)

Spots on upper wings = D and H (satin stitch)

Lower edge of upper wings = D and G (split stitch)

Lower wings on left hand butterfly = B (long and short stitch, satin stitch), C (long and short stitch), G (satin stitch)

Lower wings on right hand butterfly = E (long and short stitch, satin stitch), B and C (long and short stitch), G (satin stitch)

Stripes on lower wings = G (split stitch)

Veins = E (straight stitch, split stitch)

Body

Outlines = F (split stitch)

Thorax = F and G (satin stitch)

Thorax outline = C (split stitch)

Abdomen = F (satin stitch)

Markings on abdomen = A (straight stitch)

Divisions on abdomen = G (split stitch)

Eyes = G (padded satin stitch), H (seed stitch)

Antennae = F (back stitch, straight stitch)

Did you know?

During the 17th century in southern France making decorative petticoats and other clothing became a popular folk art. These crafted pieces were heavily quilted with floral and geometric designs. The petticoats were not hidden, instead the dresses were draped in such a way that the beautiful quilted petticoat could be seen across the front of the skirt.

14. QUEEN CRACKER

All embroidery is worked with the no. 10 sharp needle. Use the photograph as a guide to thread colour changes within the design.

Wings

Outline all four wings with split stitch and fill with long and short stitch. Using several straight stitches for each one, embroider the spots over the previous stitching.

Body

Outline the body in the same manner as the wings. Fill the body with stitches that run along the length for padding. Cover the padding with satin stitches that lie across the body. Add tiny straight stitches to form the body markings. Stitch the antennae with back stitch, finishing with several straight stitches close together for the clubbed ends.

THREADS AND NEEDLE FOR QUEEN CRACKER

Madeira stranded silk

A = 0806 dark antique violet
B = 1003 sky blue
C = 1107 Williamsburg blue
D = 1914 coffee brown
E = 2012 dark old gold
F = 2210 light tobacco
G = 2213 dark topaz
H = 2400 black

No. 10 sharp needle

EMBROIDERY KEY FOR QUEEN CRACKER

All embroidery is worked with one strand unless otherwise specified.

Wings

Outlines = H (split stitch)

Upper wings = H (long and short stitch)

Spots on upper wings = A and C (straight stitch)

Lower wings = A, D, E, F, G and H (long and short stitch)

Spots on lower wings = B and C (straight stitch)

Body

Outlines = H (split stitch)

Body = H (padded satin stitch)

Markings on body = B and C (straight stitch)

Antennae = H (back stitch, straight stitch)

15. TIGER SWALLOWTAIL

All embroidery is worked with the no. 10 sharp needle. Use the photograph as a guide to thread colour changes within the design.

Wings

Using the black thread, outline all four wings with split stitch. Embroider the black sections of the wings first and then fill in with the remaining colours. Work the veins with long split stitches. Add the topaz spots with several straight stitches close together over the previous stitching.

Body

Outline the body in the same manner as the wings. Fill the body with stitches that run along the length for padding. Cover the padding with satin stitches that lie across the body. Define the body with topaz back stitches and work several straight stitches for markings. Add a fly stitch to the head to define the eyes. Stitch the antennae with back stitch and finish with several straight stitches close together for the clubbed ends.

THREADS AND NEEDLE FOR TIGER SWALLOWTAIL

Madeira stranded silk

A = 0113 light tangerine
B = 0114 tangerine
C = 2211 topaz
D = 2400 black

No. 10 sharp needle

EMBROIDERY KEY FOR TIGER SWALLOWTAIL

All embroidery is worked with one strand unless otherwise specified.

Wings

Outlines = C and D (split stitch)

Upper wings = A, B and C (long and short stitch), D (long and short stitch, satin stitch)

Lower wings = A, B and D (long and short stitch)

Veins = D (long and short stitch)

Spots = C (straight stitch)

Body

Outlines = D (split stitch), C (back stitch)

Body = D (padded satin stitch)

Marking on head = C (fly stitch)

Markings on body = C (straight stitch)

Antennae = D (back stitch, straight stitch)

16. GREEN SWALLOWTAIL

All embroidery is worked with the no. 10 sharp needle. Use the photograph as a guide to thread colour changes within the design.

Wings

Outline all four wings with split stitch. Embroider the dark brown sections of the wings mainly with satin stitch. Use long and short stitch only where the distance to be travelled is too long for a single stitch.

Change to the emerald green thread and embroider the remainder of the wings with satin stitch, working the large area of green on each upper wing with four separate segments and the large area of green on each lower wing with three separate segments. Stitch the blue satin stitch spots on the upper wings over the previous stitching and add the veins with back stitch. Repeat for the terracotta spots near the back of the lower wings.

Add seven French knots along the wings on each side of the body for tiny spots.

Body

Outline the body in the same manner as the wings. Stitch the body with long and short stitch and the head with satin stitch. Embroider the stripes with back stitch. Add two tiny blue seed stitches for the eyes. Using the same thread, work the blue markings in each body segment, finishing with a fly stitch around the base of the abdomen. Stitch the antennae with back stitch and then work several straight stitches close together for the clubbed ends.

THREADS AND NEEDLE FOR GREEN SWALLOWTAIL

Madeira stranded silk

A = 0402 medium terracotta

B = 1003 sky blue

C = 1214 emerald green

D = 2004 black-brown

No. 10 sharp needle

EMBROIDERY KEY FOR GREEN SWALLOWTAIL

All embroidery is worked with one strand unless otherwise specified.

Wings

Outlines = D (split stitch)

Upper wings = D (long and short stitch, satin stitch), C (satin stitch)

Lower wings = D (long and short stitch, satin stitch), C (satin stitch)

Veins on upper wings = B (back stitch)

Blue spots on upper wings = B (satin stitch)

Terracotta spots on lower wings = A (satin stitch)

Tiny spots near body = A (French knot, 1 wrap)

Body

Outlines = A (split stitch)

Body = A (long and short stitch)

Stripes on body = D (back stitch)

Blue markings on body = B (straight stitch, fly stitch)

Head = D (satin stitch)

Eyes = B (seed stitch)

Antennae = D (back stitch, straight stitch)

17. ORANGE ALBATROSS

All embroidery is worked with the no. 10 sharp needle. Use the photograph as a guide to thread colour changes within the design.

Wings

Outline all four wings with split stitch. Beginning at the outer edge and working towards the body, fill the upper wings with long and short stitch. Using the brown thread, stitch several straight stitches of varying lengths near the body.

Using the mahogany thread, work the lower wings in a similar manner. Add the veins, using a combination of straight and long split stitches.

Body

Outline the body in the same manner as the wings. Fill the body with stitches that run along the length for padding. Cover the padding with satin stitches that lie across the body. Embroider straight stitches on one side of the body for markings. Add two French knots for the eyes. Stitch the antennae with back stitch and finish with several straight stitches close together for the clubbed ends.

THREADS AND NEEDLE FOR ORANGE ALBATROSS

Madeira stranded silk

A = 1914 coffee brown

B = 2008 brown

C = 2012 dark tan

D = 2213 dark topaz

E = 2306 mahogany

No. 10 sharp needle

EMBROIDERY KEY FOR ORANGE ALBATROSS

All embroidery is worked with one strand unless otherwise specified.

Wings

Upper wing outlines = D (split stitch)

Upper wings = D and E (long and short stitch), B (straight stitch)

Lower wing outlines = E (split stitch)

Lower wings = D and E (long and short stitch), B and C (straight stitch)

Veins = A (straight stitch, split stitch)

Body

Outlines = B (split stitch)

Body = B (padded satin stitch)

Markings on body = A (straight stitch)

Marking on head = A (fly stitch)

Eyes = A (French knot, 2 wraps)

Antennae = A (back stitch, straight stitch)

18. RAJAH BROOKE'S BIRDWING

All embroidery is worked with the no. 10 sharp needle. Use the photograph as a guide to thread colour changes within the design.

Wings

Outline all four wings with split stitch. Using satin stitch and the black thread, embroider the zigzag pattern along the back edge of the upper wings. Change to the light green thread and work the green triangles. Fill the remainder of the wings with long and short stitch. Add a single straight stitch along the centre of each green triangle.

Embroider the lower wings with long and short stitch, and then add the veins with a combination of long split and straight stitches.

Body

Outline the body in the same manner as the wings. Stitch the head and thorax with satin stitches that lie across the body. Embroider the red spot by working several straight stitches with the garnet thread, then several more with the shell pink thread.

Fill the abdomen with stitches that run along the length for padding. Cover the padding with satin stitches that lie in the opposite direction. Finish the abdomen with four black stripes and a fly stitch around the end. Finally, embroider the antennae with back stitch and finish with several straight stitches close together for the clubbed ends.

THREADS AND NEEDLE FOR RAJAH BROOKE'S BIRDWING

Madeira stranded silk

A = 0511 medium garnet
B = 0811 dark shell pink
C = 1408 avocado green
D = 1409 light avocado green
E = 1914 coffee brown
F = 2004 black-brown
G = 2400 black
No. 10 sharp needle

EMBROIDERY KEY FOR RAJAH BROOKE'S BIRDWING

All embroidery is worked with one strand unless otherwise specified.

Wings

Outlines = G (split stitch)

Upper wings = G (long and short stitch, satin stitch), D (satin stitch), C (straight stitch)

Lower wings = C, D, F and G (long and short stitch)

Veins on lower wings = G (split stitch, straight stitch)

Body

Outlines = G (split stitch)

Head = G (satin stitch)

Marking on head = A and B (straight stitch)

Thorax = G (satin stitch)

Abdomen = E (padded satin stitch)

Stripes on abdomen = G (straight stitch)

End of abdomen = G (fly stitch)

Antennae = G (back stitch, straight stitch)

19. PAIR OF ADONIS BLUES

All embroidery is worked with the no. 10 sharp needle. Use the photograph as a guide to thread colour changes within the design. Both butterflies are stitched in exactly the same manner, except the lower butterfly has two light coloured spots near the front of the upper wings.

Wings

Outline all four wings with split stitch. Embroider the edges with satin stitch and then fill in the remainder of each wing with long and short stitch. Use the navy thread to embroider the darker sections near the body with straight stitches of varying lengths.

Using the black thread, work a split stitch stripe along the inner edge of each white stripe. Add the veins with long split and straight stitches.

On the lower butterfly, work a spot of three straight stitches near the body on the front of each upper wing.

Body

Outline the body in the same manner as the wings. Fill the body with stitches

that run along the length for padding. Cover the padding with satin stitches that lie across the body. Stitch the antennae with back stitch and finish with several straight stitches close together for the clubbed ends.

THREADS AND NEEDLE FOR PAIR OF ADONIS BLUES

Madeira stranded silk

A = 1003 sky blue
B = 1005 dark sky blue
C = 1007 navy
D = 2400 black
E = 2401 white
No. 10 sharp needle

EMBROIDERY KEY FOR PAIR OF ADONIS BLUES

All embroidery is worked with one strand unless otherwise specified.

Wings

Outlines = B (split stitch)

Upper wings = B (long and short stitch), C (long and short stitch, straight stitch), E (satin stitch)

Lower wings = B (long and short stitch), C (long and short stitch, straight stitch), E (satin stitch)

Stripe = D (split stitch)

Veins = D (straight stitch, split stitch)

Light spots on lower butterfly = A (straight stitch)

Body

Outlines = D (split stitch)

Body = D (padded satin stitch)

Antennae = D (back stitch, straight stitch)

20. BLOMFILD'S BEAUTY

All embroidery is worked with the no. 10 sharp needle. Use the photograph as a guide to thread colour changes within the design.

Wings

Outline the wings with split stitch. Beginning from the outer edges and working towards the body, fill the wings with long and short stitch. Using the hazelnut brown thread, embroider the veins with long split stitches and add a fan of several straight stitches on each wing near the body. Stitch three white spots near the tip of each upper wing, working them over the previous stitching.

Body

Outline the body in the same manner as the wings. Fill the body with long and short stitch and work the head with padded satin stitch. Add the stripes to the abdomen with five blanket stitches. Using the black-brown thread, stitch the markings on the upper thorax and head, defining the butterfly's eyes. Stitch the antennae with back stitch and finish with several straight stitches close together for the clubbed ends.

THREADS AND NEEDLE FOR BLOMFILD'S BEAUTY

Madeira stranded silk

A = 0113 light tangerine
B = 1804 off-white
C = 2004 black-brown
D = 2012 dark old gold
E = 2114 medium hazelnut brown
F = 2213 dark topaz
G = 2306 mahogany
H = 2400 black

No. 10 sharp needle

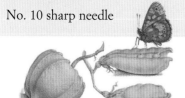

EMBROIDERY KEY FOR BLOMFILD'S BEAUTY

All embroidery is worked with one strand unless otherwise specified.

Wings

Upper wing outlines = C
(split stitch)

Lower wing outlines = D and F
(split stitch)

Upper wings = A, C, F, G and H
(long and short stitch),
E (straight stitch)

Spots on upper wings = B
(straight stitch)

Lower wings = C, D, F and G
(long and short stitch),
E (straight stitch)

Veins = E (split stitch)

Body

Outlines = D (split stitch)

Body = D and E
(long and short stitch)

Markings on thorax = C
(back stitch)

Stripes on abdomen = E
(blanket stitch)

Head = E (padded satin stitch)

Markings on head = C (back stitch)

Antennae = C
(back stitch, straight stitch)

Preparation for Quilting

Place each block face down on a well-padded surface and press.

Piecing

Lay out the blocks, four per row, and check they are correctly positioned. Using a machine straight stitch, join the blocks following the instructions on page 119.

Borders

Create the inner rust border, following the instructions on pages 122 - 123. When this border is complete, piece together the smaller patches of *Liberty* fabric for the upper and lower inner borders. Use 138 squares for each strip plus two triangles at each end to make a mitred corner. Repeat the procedure for the inner side borders using 172 squares and two triangles for each one.

Add the second rust coloured border in the same manner as the first one. Using the larger patches, create the outer pieced border in the same manner as the inner pieced border. Use 38 squares and four triangles for each upper and lower border, and 46 squares and four triangles for each side border. Press.

Layering

Assemble the lining, batting and quilt top, and baste them together following the instructions on pages 125 - 127.

Quilting

Machine quilt around every butterfly as close as possible to the edge so they stand out from the surrounding fabric.

Work the centrepiece with free motion machine quilting. Taking care not to stitch over the butterflies.

Stitch in the ditch (ie stitch along the seamline) along each side of the rust coloured border strips. Work two rows of stitching within each rust coloured strip, keeping them parallel to the edges and approximately 7mm (5/16") in from the edge.

Again using free form machine quilting, stitch four parallel rows of large waves around the outer border.

Construction

All seam allowances are 1cm (3/8") unless otherwise specified.

1. Blocking and squaring

Square the quilt following the instructions on page 135.

2. Attaching the binding

Attach the binding following the instructions on pages 138 - 139.

Children of Iceland

Photographed at Arbaer Museum,
Reykjavik, Iceland

BURST
of
SPRING

Glorious spring colours abound on this sweet quilt, perfect for a cot or to warm chilly knees on a cool evening. The central rectangle is embroidered with a garland of roses, daisies, primroses, lavender and forget-me-nots, tied at each corner with watermelon bows. Butterflies and ladybugs flit amongst the flowers. Narrow bands of striped and floral cotton border the diamonds of gently coloured *Liberty* fabrics, matched perfectly to the thread colours. The quilt is bound with a floral print and backed with a patchwork of dainty fabrics.

by Heather Scott

Requirements

Fabric

A = quilter's muslin
1.2m x 112cm wide (1yd 12" x 44")

B = check cotton
20cm x 112cm wide (8" x 44")

C = pink floral *Liberty* Tana lawn
1.9m x 112cm wide (2yd 3" x 44")

D = pink/green botanical *Liberty*
Tana lawn 25cm x 112cm wide
(10" x 44")

E = peach and pink floral *Liberty*
Tana lawn 25cm x 112cm wide
(10" x 44")

F = dusky pink and gold floral
Liberty Tana lawn 40cm x 112cm
wide (15 3/4" x 44")

G = soft green and pink floral
Liberty Tana lawn 35cm x 112cm
wide (13 3/4" x 44")

Approximately 50 small coordinating
pieces of *Liberty* Tana lawn each at
least 12cm (4 3/4") square

Embroidery threads

Gumnut yarns 'Stars' stranded silk

H = 010 very light watermelon

I = 018 dark watermelon

J = 039 very dark watermelon

K = 055 medium sweetpea

L = 174 light mulberry

M = 176 medium mulberry

N = 235 medium pansy

O = 386 medium cornflower blue

P = 389 very dark cornflower blue

Q = 406 sky blue

R = 408 dark sky blue

S = 583 light apple green

T = 587 dark apple green

U = 589 very dark apple green

V = 626 medium eucalypt

W = 643 light khaki

X = 677 dark olive

Y = 743 light daffodil

Z = 744 medium daffodil

AA = 746 dark daffodil

BB = 785 dark apricot delight

CC = 829 very dark peach Melba

DD = 857 dark salmon pink

EE = 969 dark chocolate dip

FF = 990 white

GG = 991 ecru

HH = 999 nearly black

DMC no. 8 perlé cotton

II = ecru

JJ = 3348 light yellow-green

Supplies

Cotton batting 1.1m x 120cm wide
(1yd 8" x 47 1/4")

Ecru machine sewing thread

Fine water-soluble fabric marker

Tracing paper

Sharp lead pencil

Fine black pen

Embroidery hoop
15cm (6") wide

No. 9 crewel needle

Did you know?

Quilts are often made to
commemorate events
(e.g. weddings and births) and
can incorporate pieces of fabric
from used or worn-out clothing.

Such quilts become historical
documents for the quiltmaker
and his or her loved ones.

STITCHES AND TECHNIQUES

Back stitch, Blanket stitch, Detached chain, Fly stitch
French knot, Granitos, Long and short stitch, Padded satin stitch
Running stitch, Satin stitch, Seed stitch, Stem stitch
Straight stitch, Piecing by machine, Hand quilting

The quilt measures 102.5cm x 91.5cm wide (40³/₈" x 36").

Cutting Out

See the liftout pattern sheet for the templates.

Cut a rectangle from the quilter's muslin 40.5cm x 29.5cm wide (16" x 11⁵/₈") for the embroidered centrepiece.

Cut 88 patches from the small pieces of *Liberty* Tana lawn, each 5cm (2") square. These will form 22 blocks.

From the quilter's muslin, and using the templates provided, cut thirty-six large and sixteen small triangles.

Cut out all other pieces following the instructions on the liftout pattern sheet.

Preparation for Embroidery

Transferring the designs

See the liftout pattern sheet for the embroidery designs.

Using the fine black pen, trace the centre embroidery design onto a piece of tracing paper. Tape the tracing to a window or light box. With the right side of the centrepiece facing you, centre it over the tracing. Tape in place. Using the lead pencil, trace the bow designs onto each corner, followed by the larger flowers and the butterflies. Trace the remaining flowers onto the quilter's muslin.

Trace the outer corner sprays in the same manner as before but do not transfer them onto the quilter's muslin until after the inner calico border corners have been constructed.

Embroidery

All embroidery is worked with the no. 9 crewel needle. Use the photograph as a guide to thread colour changes within the designs.

Bows

Outline the bow loops and tails of one bow with stem stitch. Repeat for the bow knot. Fill the loops, tails and centre knot with tiny seed stitches. Repeat for the remaining three corner bows.

Wild rose sprays

Embroider the petals with long and short stitch. Work 3 - 4 straight stitches for the highlights at the base of each petal in the darker pink. Change to the green thread and work a straight stitch between each petal. Fill the centre with closely packed French knots. Work the calyxes, stems and leaves next.

Stitch the petals for the side view flower, calyx and stem in the same manner as before.

Pink chrysanthemums

Embroider the petals for the flowers and buds with satin stitch. Work the stems with back stitch then the calyx of each flower with closely worked blanket stitch, radiating them from the centre of the base. Stitch the calyx for the bud with a tiny horizontal straight stitch. Embroider all the leaves with satin stitch.

White daisies

Stitch the petals for each open daisy and side-view daisy with varying lengths of closely worked straight stitches. Work vertical satin stitches for each bud. Stitch the centres of the facing flowers in the same manner as the centres of the wild roses.

Embroider the stems with back stitch and the leaves and calyxes for the buds and side-view flower with satin stitch.

Orange flowers

Embroider the little star-shaped centre of the flower with straight stitches, radiating them from the centre out. Stitch the petals with long and short stitch, using the darkest shade at the centre and the lighter shade on the outer edges. Scatter three to four tiny French knots over the darkest parts of the petals.

For the buds, work the stems with stem stitch and the leaves with satin stitch. Embroider each calyx with long and short stitch.

Work six to eight straight stitches for each petal, packing them tightly together.

Mauve sprays

Embroider the petals for the flowers and buds with satin stitch and straight stitch. Work the centre of each flower with padded satin stitch. Use the darkest part of the thread for the smaller buds.

Stitch the stems with stem stitch and then the larger leaves and calyx of each bud with satin stitch. Work the tiny leaves at the top end of the long stem with pairs of straight stitches.

The study of quilting history reveals the evolution of quilting as we know it today.

Quilts made during the early 1800s were not constructed of pieced blocks but instead whole cloth quilts, broderie perse quilts and medallion quilts were made.

Primroses

Work the petals of the flowers with long and short stitch and the buds in the same manner as those in the mauve sprays. Using the darkest shade of the daffodil thread, work a French knot in the centre of each flower and 3 - 5 tiny straight stitches radiating from the centre.

Embroider the stems, leaves and calyxes in the same manner as the mauve sprays.

Forget-me-nots

Embroider each forget-me-not with five petals. Each petal is a granitos of 8 - 10 stitches. Work a fly stitch around the tip of some of the petals and add a single French knot to the centre of each flower. Scatter groups of three detached chain leaves among the daisies.

Lavender sprigs

Each flower is embroidered in the same manner and consists of three petals. Embroider a granitos of 8 - 10 stitches for the centre petal. Work 3 - 4 straight stitches, radiating out from the base for each outer petal. Stitch a fly stitch around the tip of the centre petal. Changing to the peach Melba thread, work a tiny straight stitch between each petal.

Work straight stitches for the calyx and stitch the stems with stem stitch. Embroider the leaves with tiny straight stitches.

Butterflies

Using the close up photograph as a guide, work the spots on the upper wings with padded satin stitch.

Starting at the base, work long and short stitch, radiating outwards and changing thread colour as you stitch.

Using the green thread, work stem stitch along the front of the upper wing and satin stitch and long and short stitch around the remaining outer edge. Work a line of stem stitch to separate the upper and lower wings. Embroider the body with padded satin stitch and add tiny straight stitches for the legs and antennae. Repeat for the second butterfly.

Ladybugs

Each ladybug is worked in the same manner.

Embroider the wings with satin stitch. Work 4 - 5 tiny French knots on each wing for the spots. Stitch a straight stitch for the head and work a French knot at each end for the antennae. Stitch three small straight stitches along each side for the legs.

Corner sprays

The corner sprays are embroidered after the pieced border has been attached.

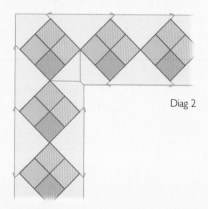

Embroider the five petals of each flower with closely worked straight stitches, working from the centre to the outer edge. Add a French knot for each centre.

Stitch the stems with stem stitch and the tiny leaves with satin stitch. Embroider the large leaves with closely worked fly stitches.

Preparation for Quilting

Place the embroidery face down on a well padded surface and press.

Piecing

Following the instructions on pages 115 - 117, and using a machine straight stitch, join four small patches together to form each block.

Join together four blocks and eight quilter's muslin triangles as shown in the diagram below (*diag 1*).

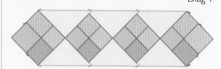

Diag 1

This will be attached to the upper end of the framed centrepiece. Repeat the procedure for the lower end and create each side with five blocks and ten quilter's muslin triangles.

Following the diagram, join the pieced strips to the remaining four blocks with small calico triangles to complete one corner (*diag 2*). Repeat for the remaining three corners.

Diag 2

Borders

Surround the embroidered centrepiece with a narrow border from the check fabric, following the instructions on pages 122 - 123. When this border is complete, repeat the procedure for the adjacent quilter's muslin border and then the outer border. Attach the framework of pieced blocks next.

For the outer border, join together a wide strip of quilter's muslin to the corresponding floral strip and then narrow quilter's muslin strip. Repeat for all remaining sides and then join the pieces together with mitres following the instructions on pages 122 - 123. Press all pieces.

Lining

Using 1cm ($3/8$") seam allowances, piece together the four rectangles of fabric according to the diagram below (*diag 3*) so they form one large rectangle 112.5cm x 101.5cm wide (44 $1/4$" x 40"). Press the seams open.

Diag 3

Layering

Assemble the lining, batting and quilt top, and baste them together following the instructions on pages 125 - 127.

Quilting

Using the green perlé cotton, work two rows of hand quilting around the checked inner border.

Using the ecru perlé cotton, quilt the remainder of the quilt in a grid pattern with lines 7.5cm (3") apart which align with the edges of the pieced blocks.

Avoid taking the lines of quilting through the embroidery and the check border.

Construction

All seam allowances are 1cm (3/8") unless otherwise specified.

1. Blocking and squaring

Square the quilt following the instructions on page 135.

2. Attaching the binding

Attach the binding following the instructions on pages 138 - 139.

Embroidery Key

All embroidery is worked with one strand unless otherwise specified.

Bows

Loops, ties and centre knot = I
(2 strands, stem stitch)

Filling = I (2 strands, seed stitch)

Wild rose sprays

Facing flowers

Petals = H
(2 strands, long and short stitch)

Petal markings = I and V
(2 strands, straight stitch)

Between petals = V
(2 strands, straight stitch)

Centre = X
(2 strands, French knot, 1 wrap)

Calyx = V (satin stitch)

Side-view flower

Petals = H
(2 strands, long and short stitch)

Calyx = V (straight stitch)

Stems and leaves

Stems = V (stem stitch)

Leaves = V (satin stitch)

Pink chrysanthemums

Flowers

Petals = K (2 strands, satin stitch)

Calyx = W (2 strands, blanket stitch)

Bud

Petals = K (2 strands, satin stitch)

Calyx = W (2 strands, straight stitch)

Stems and leaves

Stems = W (2 strands, back stitch)

Leaves = W (2 strands, satin stitch)

White daisies

Flowers

Petals = FF (2 strands, straight stitch)

Centre = AA
(2 strands, French knot, 2 wraps)

Buds

Petals = FF (2 strands, satin stitch)

Calyx = S (2 strands, satin stitch)

Stems and leaves

Stems = S (2 strands, back stitch)

Leaves = S (2 strands, satin stitch)

Orange flowers

Flower

Centre = AA (straight stitch)

Petals = CC and DD
(long and short stitch)

Petal markings = AA
(French knot, 1 wrap)

Buds

Petals = CC (straight stitch)

Calyx = U (long and short stitch)

Stems and leaves

Stems = U (stem stitch)

Leaves = U
(satin stitch, straight stitch)

Mauve sprays

Flowers

Petals = L and M
(satin stitch, straight stitch)

Centre = BB (padded satin stitch)

Buds

Petals = M
(satin stitch)

Calyx = V
(satin stitch,
straight stitch)

Stems and leaves

Stems = V
(2 strands, stem stitch)

Leaves = V
(satin stitch, straight stitch)

Primroses

Flowers

Petals = Y and Z
(long and short stitch)

Petal markings = AA (straight stitch)

Centre = AA (French knot, 2 wraps)

Buds

Petals = AA (satin stitch)

Calyx = T (satin stitch)

Stems and leaves

Stems = T (stem stitch)

Leaves = T (satin stitch)

Forget-me-nots

Flowers

Petals = O (granitos)

Petal tip = P (fly stitch)

Centre = AA (French knot, 2 wraps)

Leaves = U (detached chain)

Lavender sprigs

Flowers

Centre petal = N (granitos, fly stitch)

Outer petals = N (straight stitch)

Petal markings = CC (straight stitch)

Stems and leaves

Stems = X (stem stitch)

Leaves = X (straight stitch)

Butterflies

Spots on wing = EE
(satin stitch)

Wings = Q, R and BB
(long and short stitch)

Wing outlines = W (stem stitch,
satin stitch, long and short stitch)

Body = X (2 strands, satin stitch)

Legs = X (straight stitch)

Antennae = X (straight stitch)

Ladybugs

Wings = J (satin stitch)

Spots = HH (French knot, 1 wrap)

Head = HH (2 strands, straight stitch)

Antennae = HH
(French knot, 2 wraps)

Legs = HH (straight stitch)

Outer Sprays

Flowers

Petals = I and DD (straight stitch)

Centre = AA (French knot, 2 wraps)

Stems and leaves

Stems = T (stem stitch)

Small leaves = T (satin stitch)

Large leaves = T (fly stitch)

Quilting

Inner check border = JJ
(running stitch)

Diamond grid pattern = II
(running stitch)

Sea Shells

by Anna Scott

Fresh as a seabreeze, this delightful quilt

uses a favourite tongue twisting rhyme as its theme. Seaside colours, including sand and blue, form a background for seagulls, shells and starfish, perfectly complementing the rhyme. The central blocks are bordered with strips of teal and cream and the quilt is bound with coral fabric.

Requirements

Fabric

A = quilter's muslin 3.3m x 112cm wide (3yd 22" x 44")

B = coral shell print cotton 35cm x 112cm wide (13 3/4" x 44")

C = coral scroll print cotton 1.75m x 112cm wide (1yd 33" x 44")

D = mottled beige print cotton 35cm x 112cm wide (13 3/4" x 44")

E = beige-grey print cotton 35cm x 112cm wide (13 3/4" x 44")

F = light sand print cotton 70cm x 112cm wide (27 1/2" x 44")

G = medium sand print cotton 35cm x 112cm wide (13 3/4" x 44")

H = dark golden sand print cotton 35cm x 112cm wide (13 3/4" x 44")

I = blue and white mottled print 35cm x 112cm wide (13 3/4" x 44")

J = blue and brown mottled print cotton 35cm x 112cm wide (13 3/4" x 44")

K = mustard wave print cotton 1.4m x 112cm wide (1yd 19" x 44")

L = teal print cotton 40cm x 135cm wide (15 3/4" x 53")

Embroidery threads

DMC stranded cotton

M = ecru
N = 437 light tan
O = 598 light teal
P = 613 light taupe
Q = 640 very dark beige-grey
R = 930 dark antique blue
S = 3047 light yellow-beige
T = 3064 medium mocha
U = 3328 dark salmon
V = 3766 light peacock blue
W = 3768 dark grey-green
X = 3849 light peacock green
Y = 3864 very light latte

Anchor no. 8 perlé overdyed cotton

Z = 1302 marble

DMC no. 8 perlé cotton

AA = blanc
BB = 822 light beige-grey

Supplies

Cotton batting 1.4m x 180cm wide (1yd 19" x 70 3/4")

Ecru machine quilting thread

Fine water-soluble fabric marker

Tracing paper

Sharp lead pencil

Fine black pen

Embroidery hoop 25cm (10") wide

No. 7 crewel needle

Perfect works of art

Seashells add a beautiful touch to a home. Arrange them in a display case for an elegant look or in a specimen box for an austere appearance.

STITCHES AND TECHNIQUES

Back stitch, Blanket stitch, Chain stitch, Colonial knot, Coral stitch, Detached chain, Feather stitch, Fly stitch, French knot Running stitch, Scroll stitch, Stem stitch, Straight stitch
Piecing by machine, Straight machine quilting

The quilt measures 161.5cm x 124.5cm wide (63 ¹/₂" x 49").

Australian Wagga Quilts

The first wagga quilts were made by men who stitched together hessian flour bags with string and used them for warmth when they were away from home droving or shearing.

These bags of flour were milled at the Wagga Wagga Flour Mills in New South Wales, and so the name 'wagga' began. ('wagga' rhymes with 'jogger'). Gradually the old Australian utilitarian quilts have generally become known as waggas and even the utilitarian quilts made as recently as the 1960s and 1970s.

Cutting Out

Cut blocks from the following fabrics, each 30cm (12") square, for the embroidered blocks: A x 4, E x 2, F x 3, G x 3, H x 4, I x 4 and J x 3.

Cut blocks from the following fabrics, each 20.5cm (8") square, for the unembroidered blocks: B x 4, D x 4, E x 1, F x 2 and G x 1.

Cut out all other pieces following the instructions on the liftout pattern sheet.

Preparation for Embroidery

Transferring the designs

See the liftout pattern sheet for the embroidery designs.

Using the fine black pen, trace each embroidery design onto a separate piece of tracing paper. Tape one tracing to a window or light box. Fold the blocks into quarters and finger press the folds. With the right side of the corresponding square of fabric facing you, centre it over the tracing, matching the folds with the marked placement lines. Tape in place. Using the lead pencil, trace the design onto the fabric. Repeat for all of the embroidery designs.

Embroidery

Nautilus shells

Blocks 1, 12 and 34

Working in an anticlockwise direction, embroider a spiral of blanket stitch for each shell. Use the same hole for 5 - 7 stitches at the centre.

Sea snails

Block 5

Outline the upper cone shell with chain stitch, excluding the tip. Stitch the tip with two rows of blanket stitch and a fly stitch at the very end. Add two lines of feather stitch for markings. Changing thread colour, embroider the lower cone shell in the same manner.

Work the outlines of the two remaining shells with back stitch and then add the markings with feather stitch.

Block 17

Outline all segments of the cone shells with back stitch. Scatter detached chains within the outlines for the markings on the shells.

Stitch the outlines of the long spiral shells with chain stitch, changing to blanket stitch for the tips. Work three rows of French knots on each shell for markings.

Block 29

Embroider the cone shells in the same manner as those on block 5, omitting the fly stitch from the tip and adding a third row of blanket stitch. The long spiral shells are stitched in exactly the same manner as those on block 5.

Flying seagulls

Blocks 4, 6 and 23

Stitch the bodies, fronts of the wings and sides of the tails with stem stitch. Finish the wings and tails with blanket stitch. Create the beaks with a detached chain or a detached chain with a straight stitch below it. Embroider a colonial knot for each eye.

Standing seagulls

Blocks 9, 18, 30 and 31

Outline the bodies and wings with stem stitch. Embroider each leg with a single coral stitch, positioning the knot approximately halfway along so it forms the birds' knees. Work a fly stitch, with a short anchoring stitch, at the base of each leg for the feet.

Stitch the eyes with colonial knots and the beaks with detached chains. Add a straight stitch above each eye for eyebrows.

Starfish

Block 27

Stitch the outline with chain stitch and then work a star of five detached chains at the centre. Ensure the tip of each detached chain points towards the tip of an arm. Embroider three rows of running stitch between the tip of each detached chain at the centre and the tip of the corresponding arm.

Words

Blocks 2, 10, 11, 13, 19, 22, 25, 28 and 32

Embroider all letters with stem stitch. Dot the I's with detached chain flowers that are finished with French knot centres.

Work the waves on blocks 13, 25 and 32 with scroll stitch. Use coral stitch for the sand on the remaining blocks.

Order of blocks. Letters refer to fabric used.

Nautilus shells

Block 1

Nautilus shells = Z and AA (blanket stitch), M and S (3 strands, blanket stitch)

Block 12

Nautilus shells = Z (blanket stitch), P, Q, T and Y (3 strands, blanket stitch)

Block 34

Nautilus shells = Z (blanket stitch), M, N, S and Y (3 strands, blanket stitch)

Sea snails

Block 5

Upper cone shell outlines = N, P and S blended together (1 strand of each, chain stitch, blanket stitch, fly stitch)

Upper cone shell markings = N blended with P (1 strand of each, feather stitch)

Lower cone shell outlines = P, S and U blended together (1 strand of each, chain stitch, blanket stitch, fly stitch)

Lower cone shell markings = P blended with U (1 strand of each, feather stitch)

Left spiral shell outlines = M, P and S blended together (1 strand of each, back stitch)

Left spiral shell markings = P blended with S (1 strand of each, feather stitch)

Right spiral shell outlines = M, P and Q blended together (1 strand of each, back stitch)

Right spiral shell markings = P blended with Q (1 strand of each, feather stitch)

Block 17

Left spiral shell outlines = M (2 strands, blanket stitch, chain stitch)

Left spiral shell markings = AA (French knot, 1 wrap)

Right spiral shell outlines = M blended with S (1 strand of each, blanket stitch, chain stitch)

Right spiral shell markings = M (2 strands, French knot, 1 wrap)

Left cone shell outlines = 1 strand of U blended with 2 strands of Y (3 strands, back stitch)

Left cone shell markings = Y (2 strands, detached chain)

Right cone shell outlines = M, T and Y blended together (1 strand of each, back stitch)

Right cone shell markings = P (3 strands, detached chain)

Block 29

Upper cone shell outlines = N, T and Y blended together (1 strand of each, blanket stitch, chain stitch)

Left spiral shell outlines = N, T and U blended together (1 strand of each, back stitch)

Left spiral shell markings = N blended with T (1 strand of each, feather stitch)

Right spiral shell outlines = M, P and Y blended together (1 strand of each, back stitch)

Right spiral shell markings = M blended with P (1 strand of each, feather stitch)

Lower left cone shell outlines = M, T and Y blended together (1 strand of each, blanket stitch, chain stitch)

Lower left cone shell markings = T blended with Y (1 strand of each, feather stitch)

Lower right cone shell outlines = N, T and Y blended together (1 strand of each, blanket stitch, chain stitch)

Lower right cone shell markings = N blended with T (1 strand of each, feather stitch)

Flying seagulls

Blocks 4, 6 and 23

Bodies = AA (stem stitch)

Wings = AA
(stem stitch, blanket stitch)

Tails = AA
(stem stitch, blanket stitch)

Eyes = U (3 strands, colonial knot)

Beaks = U (3 strands,
detached chain, straight stitch)

Standing seagulls

Blocks 9, 18, 30 and 31

Bodies = AA (stem stitch)

Wings = Q (3 strands, stem stitch)

Eyes = U (3 strands, colonial knot)

Beaks = U (3 strands,
detached chain, straight stitch)

Eyebrows = Q
(2 strands, straight stitch)

Legs = U (3 strands, coral stitch)

Feet = U (3 strands, fly stitch)

Starfish

Block 27

Outline = N (4 strands, chain stitch)

Centre = T (3 strands, detached chain)

Markings = T and Y (3 strands,
running stitch)

Words

Block 2

S = V (3 strands, stem stitch)

H = O (3 strands, stem stitch)

E = X (3 strands, stem stitch)

Sand = P (3 strands, coral stitch)

Block 10

S = O (3 strands, stem stitch)

E = W (3 strands, stem stitch)

L = R (3 strands, stem stitch)

L = X (3 strands, stem stitch)

S = V (3 strands, stem stitch)

Sand = BB (coral stitch)

Block 11

S = W (3 strands, stem stitch)

E = X (3 strands, stem stitch)

A = V (3 strands, stem stitch)

Sand = S (3 strands, coral stitch)

Block 13

S = T (3 strands, stem stitch)

H = Y (3 strands, stem stitch)

E = P (3 strands, stem stitch)

L = U (3 strands, stem stitch)

L = T (3 strands, stem stitch)

S = N (3 strands, stem stitch)

Waves = Z (scroll stitch)

Block 19

S = X (3 strands, stem stitch)

I = R (3 strands, stem stitch,
French knot, 1 wrap), X (3 strands,
detached chain)

T = W (3 strands, stem stitch)

T = V (3 strands, stem stitch)

I = X (3 strands, stem stitch,
French knot, 1 wrap),
R (3 strands, detached chain)

N = W (3 strands, stem stitch)

G = O (3 strands, stem stitch)

Sand = Z (coral stitch)

Block 22

B = V (3 strands, stem stitch)

Y = W (3 strands, stem stitch)

Sand = N (coral stitch)

Block 25

T = N (3 strands, stem stitch)

H = T (3 strands, stem stitch)

E = Y (3 strands, stem stitch)

Waves = Z (scroll stitch)

Block 28

S = W (3 strands, stem stitch)

E = O (3 strands, stem stitch)

A = X (3 strands, stem stitch)

Sand = P (coral stitch)

Block 32

S = T (3 strands, stem stitch)

H = U (3 strands, stem stitch)

O = Y (3 strands, stem stitch)

R = P (3 strands, stem stitch)

E = N (3 strands, stem stitch)

Waves = Z (scroll stitch)

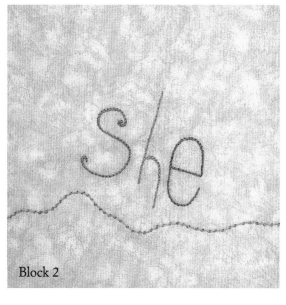

Block 2

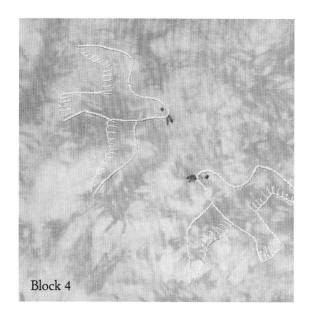

Block 4

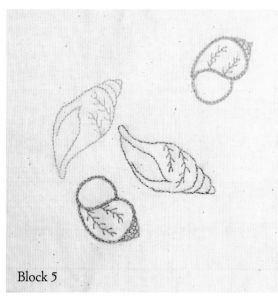

Block 5

Block 9

Block 10

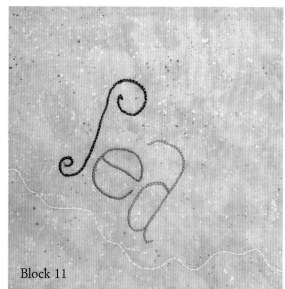

Block 11

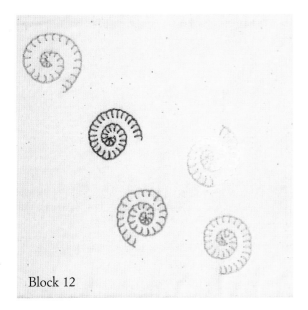

Block 12

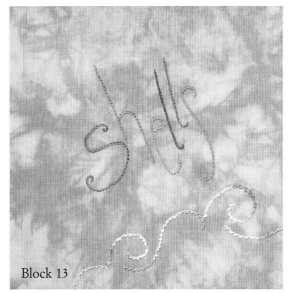

Block 13

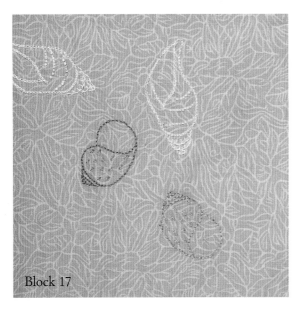

Block 17

Block 19

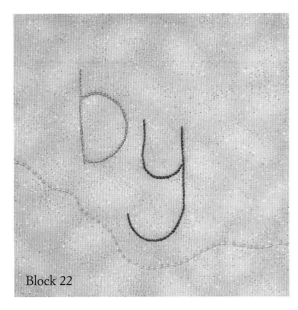

Block 22

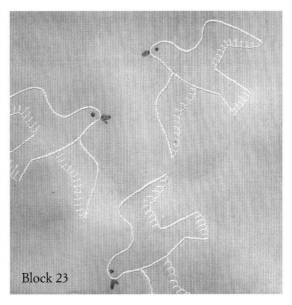

Block 23

Block 25

Block 27

Block 28

Block 29

Block 32

Block 34

68

Preparation for Quilting

Place each block face down on a well padded surface and press. Recut each embroidered block to measure 20.5cm (8") square.

Piecing

Lay out the blocks, five per row, and check they are correctly positioned. Using a machine straight stitch, join the blocks following the instructions on page 119.

Borders

Create the inner border, following the instructions on page 124. When this border is complete, repeat the procedure for the middle border and then the outer border.

Attach the two side borders to the centrepiece of the quilt lining and then the end borders. Press all pieces.

Layering

Assemble the lining, batting and quilt top, and baste them together following the instructions on pages 125 - 127.

SHE SELLS SEASHELLS,
BY THE SEASHORE.
THE SHELLS SHE SELLS,
ARE SURELY SEASHELLS.
SO IF SHE SELLS SHELLS,
ON THE SEASHORE,
I'M SURE SHE SELLS,
SEASHORE SHELLS.

Quilting

Machine quilt in the ditch (ie stitch along the seamline) between every row of blocks and then between every column of blocks to form a grid pattern.

Repeat the procedure around the outer edges of the inner and middle borders.

Construction

*All seam allowances are 1cm (3/8")
unless otherwise specified.*

1. Blocking and squaring

Block and square the quilt following the instructions on page 135.

2. Attaching the binding

Attach the binding following the instructions on pages 136 - 137.

'Making this quilt gave me the most pleasure and fun I have had stitching in a very long time.

One of my favourite scraps is printed in clear, airy, summer colours with the most curious looking seagulls on it. It gave me the idea for the beach theme. The seagulls reminded me of a book my eldest son used to love about Samantha the Seagull and so came the thought of including words. The tongue twister was short and perfect for the theme.

I usually don't like to say 'it just happened', but this quilt almost took on a life of its own. The words, the simple designs and the arrangement of the squares, quickly fell into place on my lounge room floor.' *Anna*

Botanicals

Take a quiet walk through a beautiful garden

with this superb botanical quilt. Twelve elegant flower portraits are interspersed between star blocks of vibrant floral *Liberty* fabrics. An intricate trellis of green surrounds each block creating a wonderfully decorative surface. The quilt is backed with a leaf printed cotton and bound with green and white striped fabric.

Requirements

Fabric

A = quilter's muslin 4m x 112cm wide (4yd 13 1/2" x 44")

B = green leaf print cotton 3m x 112cm wide (3yd 10" x 44")

C = green/white striped cotton 1.2m x 112cm wide (1yd 11 1/4" x 44")

D = cream leaf print cotton 4m x 112cm wide (4yd 13 1/2" x 44")

13 pieces floral *Liberty* Tana lawn, each 14cm x 30cm wide (5 1/2" x 11 3/4")

Embroidery threads and needle

See pages 75 - 85.

Supplies

Cotton batting 2m x 200cm wide (2yd 7" x 79")

Ecru machine quilting thread

Fine water-soluble fabric marker

Tracing paper

Template plastic 30cm x 40cm wide (12" x 15 3/4")

Sharp lead pencil

Fine black pen

Embroidery hoop 15cm (6") wide

Cutting Out

See the liftout pattern sheet for the templates.

Cut twelve blocks from the quilter's muslin, each 30cm (11 3/4") square, for the embroidered blocks.

Trace the templates on the liftout pattern sheet onto the template plastic and cut out. Following the instructions on the liftout pattern sheet, transfer and cut out the desired number of shapes from the corresponding fabric.

Fabulous Liberty

Liberty Tana lawn is a very British traditional fabric, 100% pure cotton, with a very fine thread count. Some of the designs are very old, some are modern, but they are all essentially Liberty. This fabric is perfect for patchwork and quilting, and lovely for little girl's hand-smocked dresses.

Tana lawn was originally made from cotton grown on the shores of Lake Tana in Ethiopia, hence the name.

In 1975 Liberty celebrated its centenary. This was heralded by a major exhibition at the Victoria and Albert Museum.

E m b r o i d e r e d   b y   C a r o l   H a w k i n s   a n d   q u i l t e d   b y   L y n   H u g h e s

The quilt measures 184cm (72 1/2") square.

Preparation for Embroidery

Transferring the designs

See the liftout pattern sheet for the embroidery designs.

Using the fine black pen, trace each embroidery design onto a separate piece of tracing paper. Tape one tracing to a window or light box. With the right side of a square of quilter's muslin facing you, centre it over the tracing. Tape in place. Using the lead pencil, trace the design onto the fabric. Repeat the procedure for the remaining eleven embroidery designs.

Embroidery

BLOCK 2
FUCHSIA

All embroidery is worked with the no. 10 sharp needle. Use the photograph as a guide to thread colour changes within the design.

Stems

Starting at the base of the main stem, work the first 2cm (3/4") with long and short stitch, and then change to satin stitch. As the smaller stems branch out from the main stem, work the lower part in satin stitch, changing to stem stitch as the stems narrow.

Using the variegated rose thread, begin working stem stitch along the side of the satin stitched section of the stem on the right. Where the stem changes to stem stitch, whip the stem stitches to the top of the stem. Repeat the procedure for the adjacent stem. Whip the stem on the left and the small stem growing from the larger middle stem.

Embroider the stems of the flowers, bud and any unattached leaves with stem stitch.

Leaves

Beginning at the base of one leaf, work each half with satin stitch, and then add the centre vein with back stitch. Embroider all remaining leaves in the same manner, working some with the lighter green thread and some with the darker green thread.

Fuchsias

Flower on left

Outline the sepals with back stitch. Beginning at the top, fill in each section with long and short stitch. Work six long straight stitches with a small bullion knot at the end of each one for the stamens.

Flower on right

Embroider the flower in the same manner as the flower on the left, adding a small satin stitch petal peeping from behind the sepals.

Bud

Stitch the petals with satin stitch. Embroider the sepals over the previous stitching with satin stitch.

THREADS AND NEEDLE FOR FUCHSIA

DMC stranded cotton

A = 99 variegated rose
B = 370 medium verdigris
C = 371 verdigris
D = 602 medium cranberry
E = 917 dark fuchsia
F = 3362 dark pine green
G = 3363 medium pine green

Madeira stranded silk

H = 0511 medium garnet
I = 0703 cranberry

Au Ver à Soie, Soie d'Alger

J = 2934 medium dusty rose
No. 10 sharp needle

EMBROIDERY KEY FOR FUCHSIA

All embroidery is worked with one strand unless otherwise specified.

Stems

Main stem = B and C
(long and short stitch)

Leaf stems = B and C
(satin stitch, stem stitch),
A (stem stitch, whipping)

Flower stems = H (stem stitch)

Bud stem = H (stem stitch)

Leaves

Filling = F and G (satin stitch)

Veins = A (back stitch)

Fuchsias

Large flowers

Sepals = D, H, I and J
(long and short stitch)

Petal (right flower only) = E
(satin stitch)

Stamens = D (straight stitch),
E (bullion knot, 4 wraps)

Bud

Sepals = H
(satin stitch, straight stitch)

Petals = E (satin stitch)

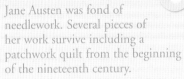

Jane Austen's Quilt

Jane Austen was fond of needlework. Several pieces of her work survive including a patchwork quilt from the beginning of the nineteenth century.

In 1811, in a letter to her sister, Cassandra, Jane asked, "have you remembered to collect pieces for the Patchwork? - we are at a standstill."

STITCHES AND TECHNIQUES

Back stitch, Bullion knot, Couching, Detached chain, Encroaching stem stitch, French knot, Granitos, Long and short stitch, Padded satin stitch, Pistil stitch, Satin stitch, Seed stitch, Split stitch Stem stitch, Straight stitch, Whipping, Piecing by hand, Piecing by machine, Straight machine quilting

BLOCK 4
LAVENDER

All embroidery is worked with the no. 10 sharp needle. Use the photograph as a guide to thread colour changes within the design.

Stems

Using the darker shade on the left hand side and the lighter shade on the right, stitch the stem to the flower head with closely worked rows of stem stitch. Embroider the base of the remaining stem with long and short stitch. Finishing approximately 15mm (5/8") from the bud, work two rows of stem stitch, side by side, for the bud's stem. Stitch the last section with encroaching stem stitch. Work the remaining stem with two rows of stem stitch as before.

Leaves

Stitch all leaves with slanting satin stitches. Use both shades of the blue-green thread, stitching some leaves with the lighter shade, some with the darker shade and some with both shades. When using both shades for a leaf, use the darker shade for the lower section and the lighter shade for the upper section.

Lavender

Large flower head

Embroider the smaller flowers with satin stitch and the larger ones with long and short stitch, changing to green thread for the sepals.

Bud

Stitch the petals first, using the light antique violet thread and satin stitch. Fill in between the petals with satin stitch and straight stitch.

THREADS AND NEEDLE FOR LAVENDER

DMC stranded cotton

A = 333 very dark blue-violet

B = 340 medium blue-violet

C = 503 medium blue-green

D = 504 very light blue-green

E = 611 dark taupe

F = 926 medium grey-green

G = 927 light grey-green

H = 928 very light grey-green

I = 3746 dark blue-violet

Madeira stranded silk

J = 0806 dark antique violet

K = 0807 light antique violet

L = 0902 blue-violet

No. 10 sharp needle

EMBROIDERY KEY FOR LAVENDER

All embroidery is worked with one strand unless otherwise specified.

Stems

Large flower head stem = C, D and F (stem stitch)

Base of bud and leaf stem = C and E (long and short stitch)

Bud stem = C and G (stem stitch), D (encroaching stem stitch)

Leaf stem = C (stem stitch)

Leaves = C and D (satin stitch)

Lavender

Large flower head

Petals = A, B, I, J, K and L (satin stitch, long and short stitch)

Sepals = C, D and H (long and short stitch)

Bud

Petals = K (satin stitch)

Sepals = D (satin stitch, straight stitch)

Lavandula

Lavandula are a genus of about 25-30 species of flowering plants in the mint family. The fragrant purple flowers and buds are used in potpourris. Oil extracted from the flower is used as an antiseptic and for aromatherapy.

BLOCK 6
GEUM

All embroidery is worked with the no. 10 sharp needle. Use the photograph as a guide to thread colour changes within the design.

Stems and leaves

Beginning at the base, work the main stems with encroaching stem stitch. Gradually taper to stem stitch for the small upper stems. Add the leaves with satin stitch, working one half before beginning the next.

Flowers

Beginning at the outer edge with the lighter thread and working towards the centre, embroider each petal with long and short stitch. Using the machine sewing thread, add the petal markings with long straight stitches. Work a padded satin stitch spot for the centre and add black straight stitches for the stamens. Scatter tiny seed stitches for the pollen on the tips of the stamens. Repeat for the second flower.

Buds

Using the hunter green thread, work the buds with satin stitch. Change to the medium yellow-green thread and using satin stitch, embroider the sepals around each bud.

THREADS AND NEEDLE FOR GEUM

DMC stranded cotton

A = 310 black

B = 349 dark coral

C = 471 very light avocado green

D = 725 dark golden yellow

E = 3346 hunter green

F = 3347 medium yellow-green

G = 3348 light yellow-green

H = 3801 very dark melon

Machine sewing thread

I = very dark red

No. 10 sharp needle

EMBROIDERY KEY FOR GEUM

All embroidery is worked with one strand unless otherwise specified.

Flowers

Petals = B and H
(long and short stitch)

Petal markings = I (straight stitch)

Centres = G (padded satin stitch)

Stamens = A (straight stitch)

Pollen = D (seed stitch)

Calyx = E, F and G
(satin stitch, straight stitch)

Buds

Petal = E (satin stitch)

Calyx = F (satin stitch)

Foliage

Stems = C (encroaching stem stitch, stem stitch)

Leaves = F or G (satin stitch)

Geum

Geum is a genus of about 50 species of perennial herbaceous plants in the rose family Rosaceae, native to Europe, Asia, North and South America, Africa and New Zealand. They are closely related to Potentilla and Fragaria.

**BLOCK 8
ST JOHN'S WORT**

All embroidery is worked with the no. 10 sharp needle. Use the photograph as a guide to thread colour changes within the design.

Stems and leaves

Embroider the multicoloured leaves first, stitching each one from the centre. Change to the terracotta thread and embroider the two main stems with encroaching stem stitch. Work a line of stem stitch with green silk on the left hand side of each stem.

Join any unattached leaves to the main stems with short stalks of straight stitch or stem stitch.

Flower

Beginning at the outer edge and working towards the centre, embroider each petal with long and short stitch. Gradually change from the lightest shade to the darkest as you work.

Stitch the stamens with pistil stitches that radiate from the centre. Work a satin stitch spot at the centre, then add four bullion knots over the stamens.

Large bud

Stitch the petal on the left with satin stitch and the remaining two petals with long and short stitch. Add the sepals with satin stitch.

Small buds

Work the stems first using stem stitch. Embroider the petals of the buds with padded satin stitch. Work each sepal with satin stitch, completing one before starting the next. Partially outline the sepals of the bud on the left with terracotta straight stitches.

THREADS AND NEEDLE FOR ST JOHN'S WORT

DMC stranded cotton

A = 356 medium terracotta

B = 725 dark golden yellow

C = 726 golden yellow

D = 727 light golden yellow

E = 745 very light yellow

F = 3348 light yellow-green

G = 3716 very light dusky rose

H = 3733 dusky rose

I = 3823 ultra light yellow

Gumnut Yarns 'Stars' stranded silk

J = 589 very dark apple green

No. 10 sharp needle

EMBROIDERY KEY FOR ST JOHN'S WORT

All embroidery is worked with one strand unless otherwise specified.

Flower

Petals = B, C and D
(long and short stitch)

Centre = F (satin stitch, bullion knot, 4 - 6 wraps)

Stamens = E (pistil stitch)

Large bud

Petals = B (satin stitch),
C (long and short stitch, satin stitch)

Sepals = F (satin stitch)

Small buds

Petals of bud on left = E
(padded satin stitch)

Petals of middle bud = C
(padded satin stitch)

Petals of bud on right = C
(padded satin stitch)

Sepals = F (satin stitch)

Markings on sepals of left bud = H (straight stitch)

Foliage

Main stems = A and J (encroaching stem stitch, stem stitch)

Bud stems = F and J (stem stitch)

Leaf stems = A and J
(stem stitch, straight stitch)

Leaves = G, H, I and J
(satin stitch)

St John's Wort

St John's Wort refers to the species Hypericum perforatum, also known as Klamath weed or Goat weed. The common name comes from the fact that it traditionally flowers by and is harvested on St John's day, 24 June. The first recorded use of Hypericum for medicinal purposes dates back to ancient Greece. In modern medicine, it is commonly used as a treatment for depression and anxiety disorders.

BLOCK 10
GERANIUM

All embroidery is worked with the no. 10 sharp needle. Use the photograph as a guide to thread colour changes within the design.

Stems and leaves

Beginning at the base, work the main stem first, using stem stitch for the right hand side and encroaching stem stitch, tapering to stem stitch, for the left hand side. Embroider the leaf and flower stems with stem stitch. Work a section of satin stitch at the base of the bud stems before completing them with stem stitch.

Back stitch the main parts of the leaves and then embroider the remaining parts with straight stitches.

Flowers and buds

Beginning at the outer edge and working towards the centre, embroider each petal of the facing flower with long and short stitch. Grade from the lighter shade on the outside to the darker shade near the centre. Fill the centre with ecru long and short stitches. Add a star shape of five straight stitches at the very centre.

Using the lighter violet thread, stitch the petals of the side-view flower with long and short stitch. Change to the pine green thread and work the sepals in the same manner.

Finally, add each bud with long and short stitch.

THREADS AND NEEDLE FOR GERANIUM

DMC stranded cotton

A = ecru
B = 552 medium violet
C = 553 violet
D = 841 light beige

E = 3053 green-grey
F = 3346 hunter green
G = 3364 pine green
H = 3830 terracotta
No. 10 sharp needle

EMBROIDERY KEY FOR GERANIUM

All embroidery is worked with one strand unless otherwise specified.

Facing flower

Petals = B and C
(long and short stitch)

Centre = A (long and short stitch), H (straight stitch)

Side-view flower

Petals = C (long and short stitch)

Sepals = G (long and short stitch)

Buds = E (long and short stitch)

Foliage

Main stem = D (encroaching stem stitch, stem stitch), G (stem stitch)

Flower stems = G (stem stitch)

Leaf stems = E, F and G
(stem stitch)

Bud stems = E and G
(stem stitch, satin stitch)

Leaves = F and G
(back stitch, straight stitch)

Pelargonium

A genus of flowering plants that includes about 200 species of perennial, succulent, and shrub plants, commonly known as geraniums. The shapes of the flowers range from star-shaped to funnel-shaped, and colors include white, pink, red, orange-red, fuchsia to deep purple. They are extremely popular garden plants, grown as annuals in temperate climates, and thousands of ornamental cultivars have been developed from about 20 of the species.

BLOCK 12
BEGONIA

All embroidery is worked with the no. 10 sharp needle. Use the photograph as a guide to thread colour changes within the design.

Stems and leaves

Beginning at the base, work the stems with satin stitch and encroaching stem stitch. Embroider the large and medium leaves with satin stitch and then add the centre veins with back stitch. On the four large leaves, add 4 - 5 straight stitches for markings.

Stitch the two small leaves with satin stitch. Using the same thread, work the partial outlines along the upper stems with back stitch.

Flowers

Both flowers are worked in a similar manner. Embroider the sepals and then the petals with long and short stitch, completing one petal before beginning the next. To work the stamens, stitch several straight stitches and then add 3 - 4 French knots at the end.

Buds

Work the buds in a similar manner to the flowers, omitting the stamens.

THREADS AND NEEDLE FOR BEGONIA

DMC stranded cotton

A = blanc
B = 725 dark golden yellow
C = 772 very light yellow-green
D = 818 baby pink
E = 819 light baby pink
F = 963 ultra light dusky rose
G = 3346 hunter green
H = 3347 medium yellow-green
I = 3712 medium salmon
J = 3716 very light dusky rose
No. 10 sharp needle

EMBROIDERY KEY FOR BEGONIA

All embroidery is worked with one strand unless otherwise specified.

Flower on left

Petals = A, D, F and J
(long and short stitch)

Stamens = B (straight stitch,
French knot, 2 wraps)

Sepals = I and J
(long and short stitch)

Flower on right

Petals = A, E, F and J
(long and short stitch)

Stamens = B (straight stitch,
French knot, 2 wraps)

Sepals = A and I
(long and short stitch)

Upper bud

Petals = A, D, F and J
(long and short stitch)

Sepals = C, I and J
(long and short stitch)

Lower bud

Petals = A, D, E, F and J
(long and short stitch)

Sepals = I and J
(long and short stitch)

Stems

Stems = I
(encroaching stem stitch)

Partial outlines on upper stems
= C (back stitch)

Large leaves

Leaves = G and H (satin stitch)

Leaf markings = I (straight stitch)

Centre veins = I (back stitch)

Medium leaves

Leaves = G and H (satin stitch)

Centre veins = I (back stitch)

Small leaves = C (satin stitch)

BLOCK 14
VIOLETS

All embroidery is worked with the no. 10 sharp needle. Use the photograph as a guide to thread colour changes within the design.

Stems and leaves

Beginning at the base, work the three main stems with satin stitch and encroaching stem stitch. Gradually taper to stem stitch for the upper sections. Add the leaves with satin stitch and the leaf buds with stem and satin stitch.

Flowers

All the flowers are stitched in a similar manner.

Beginning at the outer edge and working towards the centre, embroider each petal with long and short stitch. Gradually change from the lightest shade to the darkest as you work. Overlay some of the petals with straight stitches.

Using the old gold thread, stitch 2 - 3 straight stitches for the centres. Surround these with white straight stitch highlights.

THREADS AND NEEDLE FOR VIOLETS

DMC stranded cotton

A = 550 very dark violet

B = 552 medium violet

C = 553 violet

D = 554 light violet

Gumnut Yarns 'Stars' stranded silk

E = 549 very dark forest green

F = 589 very dark apple green

Madeira stranded silk

G = 1408 avocado green

H = 2209 old gold

I = 2401 white

No. 10 sharp needle

EMBROIDERY KEY FOR VIOLETS

All embroidery is worked with one strand unless otherwise specified.

Flowers

Petals = A, B and C (long and short stitch), D (long and short stitch, straight stitch)

Centres = H (straight stitch)

Centre highlights = I (straight stitch)

Calyx = E, F and G (satin stitch, straight stitch)

Bud

Petal = B (satin stitch)

Calyx = F (straight stitch)

Foliage

Stems = E, F and H (encroaching stem stitch, satin stitch, stem stitch)

Leaves = E or F (satin stitch)

Leaf buds = E, F and G (satin stitch, stem stitch)

Violets

- Violets (viola) are small perennial plants, but a few are annual plants and some are small shrubs.
- The culinary use of violets can be dated back to 140 B.C.
- They can be crystallised and used as cake decorations, as well as being used to flavour salads and desserts.
- One quirk of some violets is the elusive scent of their flowers; a major component of the scent is a compound called ionone, which temporarily desensitises the receptors in the nose.

Block 2
Fuchsia

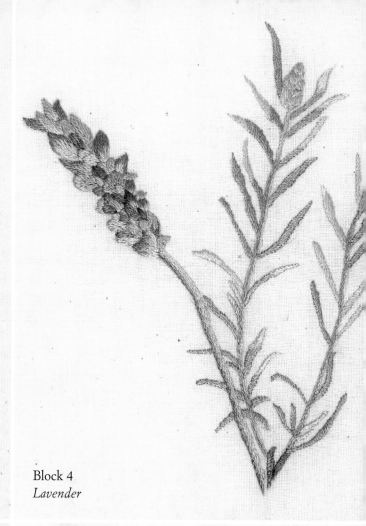

Block 4
Lavender

Block 6
Geum

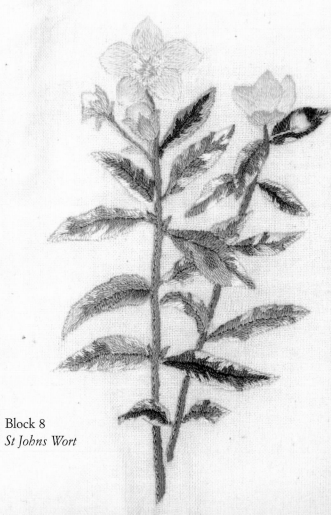

Block 8
St Johns Wort

Block 10
Geranium

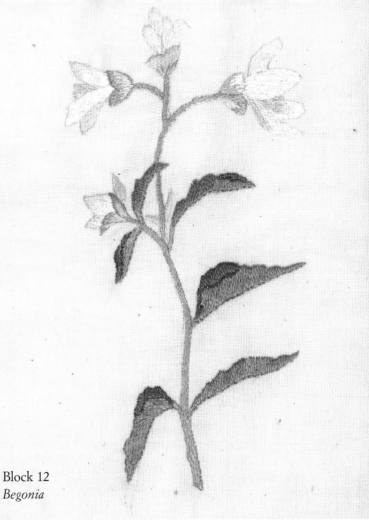

Block 12
Begonia

Block 14
Violets

Block 16
Pansies

Block 18
Alyssum

Block 20
Buddleia

Block 22
Honeysuckle

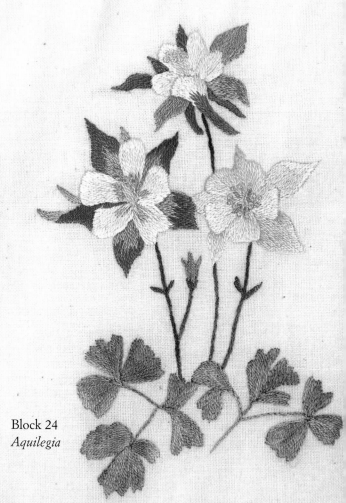

Block 24
Aquilegia

BLOCK 16
PANSIES

All embroidery is worked with the no. 10 sharp needle. Use the photograph as a guide to thread colour changes within the design.

Foliage

Beginning at the base, work the main stems with encroaching stem stitch, gradually tapering to stem stitch for the upper sections. Add the leaves with satin stitch. Work the stems for the buds with stem stitch.

Flowers

Starting at the outer edge and working towards the centre, embroider the two upper petals of each flower with long and short stitch. Work the lower petal next, followed by the two side petals.

Stitch the centre of each flower with vertical satin stitches. Embroider radiating straight stitches on the lower and side petals for markings. Work 2 - 3 straight stitches on each side of the centre, forming an inverted 'V'.

Buds

Embroider the petals with satin stitch, then work the calyxes with straight stitches of varying lengths.

THREADS AND NEEDLE FOR PANSIES

DMC stranded cotton

A = 743 yellow
B = 745 very light yellow
C = 746 off-white
D = 972 deep canary
E = 3053 green-grey
F = 3371 black-brown
G = 3685 wine
H = 3731 very dark dusky rose
I = 3733 dusky rose
J = 3803 light wine

Gumnut Yarns 'Stars' stranded silk

K = 628 dark eucalypt
L = 629 very dark eucalypt

M = 589 very dark apple green
N = 829 very dark peach Melba

Madeira stranded silk

O = 0112 custard
P = 0811 very dark shell pink
Q = 0812 dark shell pink
R = 1407 avocado green
S = 2208 light old gold

No. 10 sharp needle

EMBROIDERY KEY FOR PANSIES

All embroidery is worked with one strand unless otherwise specified.

Flower 1

Upper petals = G and H
(long and short stitch)

Middle petals = Q and S
(long and short stitch)

Lower petal = A, D, P and Q
(long and short stitch)

Petal markings = F (straight stitch)

Centre = E (satin stitch),
C (straight stitch)

Flower 2

Upper petals = B and C
(long and short stitch)

Middle petals = B and S
(long and short stitch)

Lower petal = B, D and S
(long and short stitch)

Petal markings = P (straight stitch)

Centre = E (satin stitch),
C (straight stitch)

Flower 3

Upper petals = P, Q and S
(long and short stitch)

Middle petals = Q and S
(long and short stitch)

Lower petal = A, O and P
(long and short stitch)

Petal markings
= F (straight stitch)

Centre = E (satin stitch),
C (straight stitch)

Flower 4

Upper petals = G, H and J
(long and short stitch)

Middle petals = H and I
(long and short stitch)

Lower petal = A, I, J and N
(long and short stitch)

Petal markings = F (straight stitch)

Centre = E (satin stitch),
C (straight stitch)

Flower 5

Upper petals = G, J and O
(long and short stitch)

Middle petals = O and S
(long and short stitch)

Lower petal = A, O, P and S
(long and short stitch)

Petal markings = F (straight stitch)

Centre = E (satin stitch),
C (straight stitch)

Small buds

Petal = G (satin stitch)

Calyx = L (straight stitch)

Large bud

Petals = H and J (satin stitch)

Calyx = K (straight stitch)

Foliage

Leaves = K, L, M and R
(satin stitch)

Stems = K, L and R (encroaching
stem stitch, stem stitch)

Pansies

- The pansy is a cultivated garden flower. It is derived from a wildflower called heartsease or johnny jump up (viola tricolor).

- The pansy gets its name from the French word pensée meaning 'thought'. It was so named because the flower resembles a human face and it nods forward as if deep in thought.

- The pansy remains a favourite image in the arts and crafts, from needlepoint to ceramics.

BLOCK 18
ALYSSUM

All embroidery is worked with the no. 10 sharp needle. Use the photograph as a guide to thread colour changes within the design.

Foliage

Beginning at the base, work the main stems with encroaching stem stitch, gradually tapering to stem stitch for the upper sections. Add the leaves with satin or encroaching stem stitch and then the flower and bud stems with stem, back or straight stitch.

Flowers

Embroider each green bud with either a granitos of 2 - 3 straight stitches, a French knot or a detached chain.

Stitch each petal with either a granitos of 2 - 3 straight stitches or a detached chain. In the centre of each flower, work 1 - 2 very tiny straight stitches with the avocado green thread and then place a yellow French knot over the top.

THREADS AND NEEDLE FOR ALYSSUM

Gumnut Yarns 'Stars' stranded silk

A = 549 very dark forest green

B = 589 very dark apple green

C = 708 dark lemon crush

Madeira stranded silk

D = 1407 avocado green

Au Ver à Soie, Soie d'Alger

E = blanc

No. 10 sharp needle

EMBROIDERY KEY FOR ALYSSUM

All embroidery is worked with one strand unless otherwise specified.

Flowers

Petals = E (detached chain)

Centres = C (French knot, 1 wrap), D (straight stitch)

Buds = A or B (detached chain, granitos, French knot, 1 wrap)

Foliage

Main stems = A or B (encroaching stem stitch, stem stitch)

Flower stems = A or B (stem stitch, straight stitch)

Bud stems = A or B (back stitch, stem stitch, straight stitch)

Leaves = A or B (encroaching stem stitch, satin stitch)

BLOCK 20
BUDDLEIA

All embroidery is worked with the no. 10 sharp needle. Use the photograph as a guide to thread colour changes within the design.

Foliage

Stitch the main stem and then the two secondary stems. Embroider all the leaves with satin stitch. Work the leaf veins and outlines and then stitch the flower and bud stems.

Flowers

Embroider tiny granitos of 2 - 3 straight stitches for the petals of the flowers. Add French knot centres to most of the flowers. Work the buds using either a French knot or 1 - 2 very small straight stitches.

THREADS AND NEEDLE FOR BUDDLEIA

DMC stranded cotton

A = 319 dark pistachio green

B = 320 medium pistachio green

C = 433 medium brown

D = 520 dark fern green

E = 522 fern green

F = 524 very light fern green

G = 718 medium fuchsia

H = 721 medium orange spice

I = 3607 fuchsia

J = 3608 light fuchsia

No. 10 sharp needle

EMBROIDERY KEY FOR BUDDLEIA

All embroidery is worked with one strand unless otherwise specified.

Flowers

Petals = G, I and J (granitos)

Centres = H (French knot, 1 wrap)

Buds = G, I and J (straight stitch, French knot, 1 wrap)

Stems

Main stem = C, E and F (encroaching stem stitch, long and short stitch, satin stitch)

Secondary stems = F (satin stitch)

Flower stems = F (straight stitch, back stitch)

Bud stems = F (straight stitch)

Leaves

Large leaves = A and F (satin stitch)

Veins and outlines on large leaves = D (back stitch)

Highlight to lower left leaf = B (satin stitch)

Small leaves = A, B, E and F (satin stitch)

Buddleia

Buddleia was named after the Reverend Adam Buddle, a botanist and a rector in England. The most popular species is Buddleia davidii from central China. Other popular species include Buddleia globosa from southern Chile, grown for its strongly honey-scented flowers and medicinal uses.

BLOCK 22
HONEYSUCKLE

All embroidery is worked with the no. 10 sharp needle. Use the photograph as a guide to thread colour changes within the design.

Stems and leaves

Starting at the base, stitch the stem with satin stitch. Gradually change to encroaching stem stitch as you near the tip.

Using the two shades of moss green, embroider the leaves with satin stitch. Work along one half of the leaf, around the tip and then down the other half.

Flowers

Beginning at the base, work the petals of the open flowers with satin stitch and long and short stitch. Embroider 5 - 6 straight stitches of varying lengths for the stamens. Couch some stamens to achieve a gentle curve. Add a tiny straight stitch across the top of each one.

Work the closed flowers with satin stitch. Embroider tightly packed French knots where the base of the flowers join the stem.

THREADS AND NEEDLE FOR HONEYSUCKLE

DMC stranded cotton

A = 434 light brown

B = 435 very light brown

C = 580 dark moss green

D = 581 moss green

E = 680 dark old gold

Madeira stranded silk

F = 0112 custard

G = 2207 very light old gold

H = 2208 light old gold

I = 2209 medium old gold

Minnamurra hand-dyed stranded cotton

J = 180 straw yellow/green

No. 10 sharp needle

EMBROIDERY KEY FOR HONEYSUCKLE

All embroidery is worked with one strand unless otherwise specified.

Flowers

Petals of open flowers = B, E, G, H, I and J (satin stitch, long and short stitch)

Petals of closed flowers = G, H, I and J (satin stitch)

Stamens = F and I (straight stitch)

Base of flowers = B, E, G, H and J (French knot, 1 wrap)

Stem = A (satin stitch, encroaching stem stitch)

Leaves = C or D (satin stitch)

Honeysuckle

- There are over 180 species of honeysuckle *(Lonicera)*, the most common of which are the European, Japanese, Chinese Coral and Trumpet honeysuckles.

- *Lonicera xylosteum* (Fly Honeysuckle) is a common homeopathic remedy, used for asthma, breathing difficulties and syphilis. Lonicera periclymenum (European honeysuckle) is an uncommon homeopathic remedy, used for irritability with violent outbursts.

- According to The Language of Flowers the honeysuckle represents sweetness of disposition.

BLOCK 24
AQUILEGIA

All embroidery is worked with the no. 10 sharp needle. Use the photograph as a guide to thread colour changes within the design.

Flowers

Stitch the inner and then the outer petals with long and short stitch. Complete the petals of one flower before beginning those of the next. Add petal markings to the two lower flowers.

Work a fan shape of straight stitches of varying lengths for the stamens of the left and upper flowers. Add French knots to the tips of the straight stitches. Beginning near the centre each time, work radiating straight stitches for the stamens of the flower on the right. Add French knots to the tips of the stitches.

Foliage

Embroider the leaves, leaf stems and bud using the lighter sections of the green thread. Stitch the flower stems, small leaves and bud calyx with the darker sections of the same thread.

THREADS AND NEEDLE FOR AQUILEGIA

Gumnut Yarns 'Stars' stranded silk

A = 549 very dark forest green

Madeira stranded silk

B = 0112 custard

C = 0503 baby pink

D = 0811 very dark shell pink

E = 0812 dark shell pink

F = 0813 shell pink

G = 0815 very light shell pink

H = 2207 very light old gold

I = 2208 light old gold

J = 2209 medium old gold

No. 10 sharp needle

EMBROIDERY KEY FOR AQUILEGIA

All embroidery is worked with one strand unless otherwise specified.

Upper flower

Inner petals = B, F and G
(long and short stitch)

Outer petals = D and E
(long and short stitch)

Stamens = I (straight stitch,
French knot, 2 wraps)

Flower on left

Inner petals = F and G
(long and short stitch)

Outer petals = D and E
(long and short stitch)

Petal markings = E (straight stitch)

Stamens = I (straight stitch),
J (French knot, 2 wraps)

Flower on right

Inner petals = B and H
(long and short stitch)

Outer petals = C and F
(long and short stitch)

Petal markings = E (straight stitch)

Stamens = I (straight stitch,
French knot, 2 wraps)

Bud

Petals = A (satin stitch)

Calyx = A (straight stitch)

Foliage

Stems = A (stem stitch)

Large leaves = A
(long and short stitch)

Small leaves = A (straight stitch)

Aquilegias

• Aquilegias are also known as columbines or granny's bonnets and have been known to gardeners and artists since at least medieval times. They are found in meadows, woodlands, and at higher altitudes throughout the northern hemisphere. Known for their distinctive flowers, generally bell-shaped, each petal is modified into an elongated nectar spur.

• Several species are grown in gardens: the European Columbine, Aquilegia vulgaris, is a traditional garden flower in Britain, and several of the species that are native to North America are popular garden plants there.

• Aquilegias are used as food plants by some Lepidoptera species including Cabbage Moth, Dot Moth, the Engrailed and Mouse Moth.

Did you know?

• In 1924 archaeologists discovered a quilted floor covering in Mongolia dating back from first century BC to the second century AD.

• Quilting was brought to Europe from the Middle East by Crusaders in the 11th century.

Preparation for Quilting

Place each embroidered block face down on a well padded surface and press. Recut the blocks to measure 17cm (6 3/4") square.

Piecing

Create the star blocks following the instructions on page 89.

Using a machine straight stitch, attach first the upper and lower borders and then the side borders to each embroidered block and each star block. Lay out the blocks, five per row, and check they are correctly positioned. Beginning from the centre and working outwards attach the quilter's muslin hexagons and remaining green pieces of sashing (diag 1). Set in quilter's muslin triangles in the spaces around the edge so the sides become straight.

Borders

Create the border, following the instructions on pages 121 - 122, adding the end borders first and then the side borders. Press all pieces.

Layering

Assemble the lining, batting and quilt top, and baste them together following the instructions on pages 125 - 127.

Quilting

Machine quilt in the ditch (ie stitch along the seamline) around each block and around the outer edge of each star. Repeat the procedure around each quilter's muslin hexagon and then work two parallel rows of stitching within each hexagon, keeping the rows approximately 6mm (1/4") apart.

Stitch around the entire outer edge of the green sashing and then stitch two

more parallel rows beyond this row in the same manner as before.

Construction

All seam allowances are 1cm (3/8") unless otherwise specified.

1. Blocking and squaring

Square the quilt following the instructions on page 135.

2. Attaching the binding

Attach the binding following the instructions on pages 138 - 139.

....

Hints on Piecing

- Before cutting out all the pieces you require, make a test block to see if you like the selected fabrics together. This is also a good check for the accuracy of the pattern you are using.

- Ensure your seams are accurately stitched. Any inaccuracies magnify as you progress with your quilt top.

- Wherever possible, press seam allowances towards the darker of two fabrics. If you need to press towards the lighter fabric, trim the seam allowance on the darker fabric to ensure it is slightly narrower than the seam allowance on the lighter fabric.

- Study your block pattern to determine the simplest sewing order. Many patterns will indicate a sewing order by showing those pieces that should be joined first as lying closer together, grading to those that should be joined last as lying farthest apart.

Diag 1

piecing the star blocks

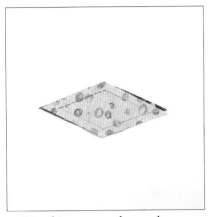

1. Matching raw edges, place two diamonds right sides together. Hand stitch along one side, taking care not to stitch in the seam allowance.

2. Repeat for the remaining pairs of diamonds. Press the seams to one side.

3. Set in a quilter's muslin triangle in the 'V' shape formed between the two diamonds.

4. Handstitch two pairs together, again taking care not to stitch in the seam allowance.

5. Set in a quilter's muslin square in the 'V' formed by the two pairs of diamonds. Attach a second square to the diamond on the right.

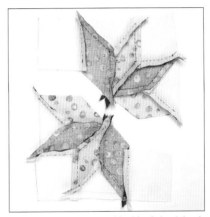

6. Create the second half of the block in exactly the same manner.

7. Place the two halves right sides together and stitch, again taking care not to stitch in the seam allowance.

8. Press the seams nearest the centre to one side ensuring all seams are pressed in the same direction.

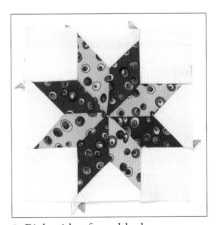

9. Right side of star block.

back stitch

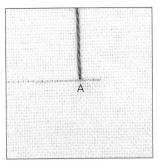

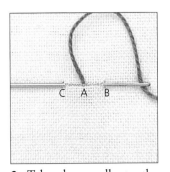

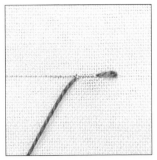

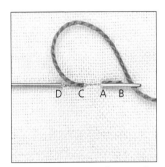

1. Secure the thread on the back of the fabric and bring it to the front at A, a short distance from the right hand end.

2. Take the needle to the back at the right hand end (B). Re-emerge at C. The distance from A to B is the same as the distance from A to C.

3. Pull the thread through to complete the first stitch.

4. Take the needle to the back at A, using exactly the same hole in the fabric as before. Re-emerge at D, on the other side of C.

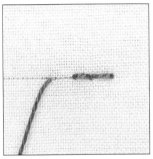

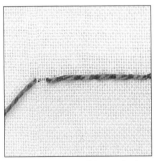

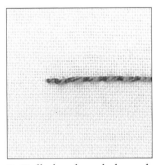

5. Pull the thread through to complete the second stitch.

6. Continue working stitches in the same manner.

7. To end off, take the needle to the back through the hole at the beginning of the previous stitch.

8. Pull the thread through and end off on the back of the fabric.

blanket stitch

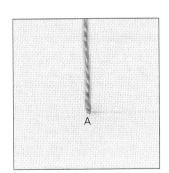

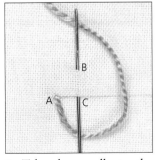

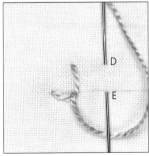

1. Secure the thread on the back of the fabric and bring it to the front at A.

2. Take the needle to the back at B and re-emerge at C. Ensure the thread is under the tip of the needle.

3. Pull the thread through until it lies snugly against the emerging thread but does not distort the fabric.

4. Take the needle to the back at D and re-emerge at E. Ensure the thread lies under the tip of the needle.

blanket stitch / continued

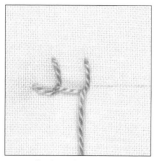

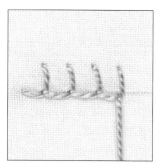

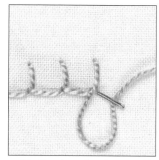

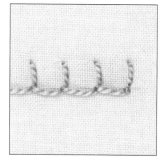

5. Pull the thread through as before.

6. Continue working stitches in the same manner.

7. To finish, take the needle to the back of the fabric just over the last loop.

8. Pull the thread through and end off on the back of the fabric.

bullion knot

↑ indicates top of fabric

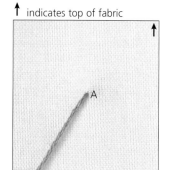

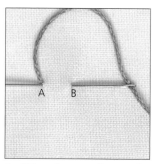

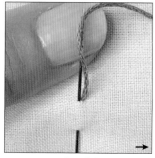

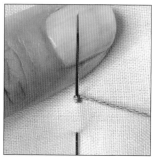

1. Secure the thread on the back of the fabric. Bring it to the front at A.

2. Take the needle to the back at B. Re-emerge at A, taking care not to split the thread.

3. Rotate the fabric. Raise the tip of the needle away from the fabric. Wrap the thread clockwise around the needle.

4. Keeping the tip of the needle raised, pull the wrap firmly down onto the fabric.

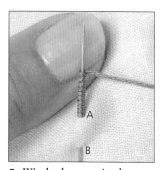

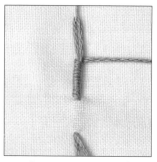

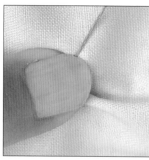

5. Work the required number of wraps around the needle. The number of wraps must cover the distance from A - B plus an extra 1 - 2 wraps. Pack them down evenly as you wrap.

6. Keeping tension on the wraps with your thumb, begin to ease the needle through the fabric and wraps.

7. Continuing to keep tension on the wraps with your thumb, pull the thread through (thumb not shown).

8. Pull the thread all the way through, tugging it away from you to form a small pleat in the fabric. This helps to ensure a tight even knot.

bullion knot / continued

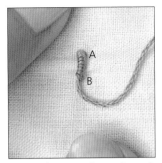

9. Release the thread. Smooth out the fabric and the knot will lie back towards B.

10. To ensure all the wraps are even, gently stroke and manipulate them with the needle while maintaining tension on the thread.

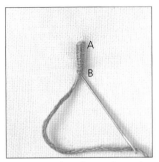

11. To finish, take the needle to the back at B.

12. Pull the thread through and end off on the back of the fabric.

chain stitch

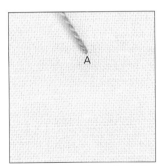

1. Secure the thread on the back of the fabric and bring it to the front at A.

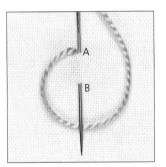

2. Take the needle from A to B, using the same hole in the fabric at A. Loop the thread under the tip of the needle.

3. Pull the thread through until the loop lies snugly against the emerging thread.

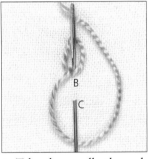

4. Take the needle through the same hole in the fabric at B and re-emerge at C. Loop the thread under the tip of the needle.

5. Pull the thread through as before.

6. Continue working stitches in the same manner.

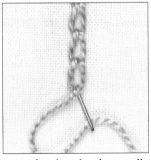

7. To finish, take the needle to the back just over the last loop.

8. Pull the thread through and end off on the back of the fabric.

colonial knot

1. Secure the thread on the back of the fabric and bring it to the front at the position for the knot.

2. Hold the thread loosely in your left hand. With your right hand, place the tip of the needle over the thread.

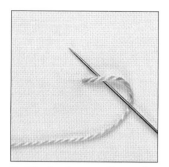

3. Hook the needle under the thread where it emerges from the fabric.

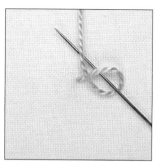

4. With your left hand, take the thread over the tip of the needle to form a loop. Shorten the loop.

5. Take the thread under the tip of the needle to form a figure eight around the needle.

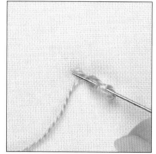

6. Take the tip of the needle to the back of the fabric approximately two fabric threads away from where the thread first emerged.

7. Pull the wraps firmly against the fabric.

8. Keeping the thread taut, push the needle through the knot to the back of the fabric.

9. Hold the knot and loop on the fabric with your thumb and continue to pull the thread through (thumb not shown).

10. Pull until the loop disappears. Secure the thread on the back of the fabric.

The Little Nut Tree, Inspirations issue 11

coral stitch

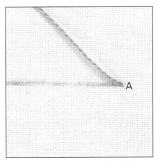

1. Draw a line on the fabric. Secure the thread on the back of the fabric and bring it to the front on the right hand end of the line (A).

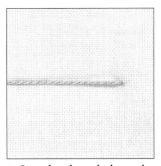

2. Lay the thread along the line and hold in place with your thumb (thumb not shown).

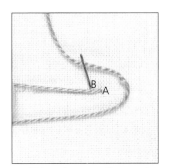

3. Take the needle to the back at B, just above the laid thread. A loop forms below the line.

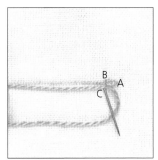

4. Still holding the thread, bring the needle to the front at C, within the loop just below B and the laid thread.

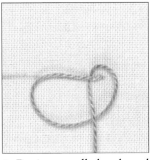

5. Begin to pull the thread through gently.

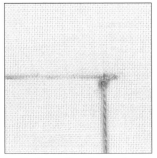

6. Pull until a knot forms against the fabric.

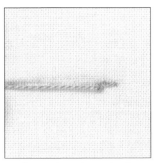

7. Lay the thread along the line again and hold in place with your thumb (thumb not shown).

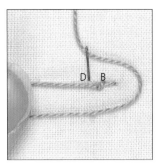

8. Take the needle to the back at D, just above the laid thread and to the left of the previous knot.

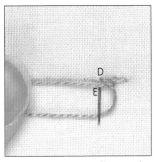

9. Bring the needle to the front at E, within the loop just below D and the laid thread.

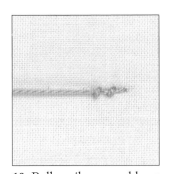

10. Pull until a second knot forms against the fabric.

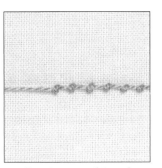

11. Continue working along the line in the same manner.

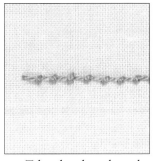

12. Take the thread to the back of the fabric and end off.

Did you know?

There is a common belief that quilting originated in utilitarianism rather than decoration. But in colonial times most women spent their days spinning, weaving and making clothing. Meanwhile women of the wealthy classes prided themselves on their fine quilting of wholecloth quilts.

couching

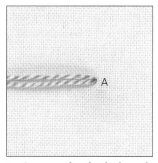

1. Secure the laid threads on the back of the fabric and bring to the front at A. Lay on the fabric.

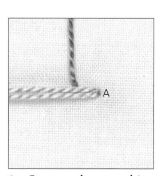

2. Secure the couching thread on the back of the fabric and bring it to the front just above the laid threads near A.

3. Take the needle over the laid threads and to the back of the fabric.

4. Pull the thread through to form the first couching stitch.

5. Bring the thread to the front just above the laid threads a short distance away from the first couching stitch.

6. Pull the thread through. Continue working stitches in the same manner for the required distance.

7. Take the couching thread to the back of the fabric and end off.

8. Take the laid threads to the back of the fabric and end off.

When to use a hoop for embroidery

Hoops are designed to hold the fabric taut while stitching, thus preventing any unsightly puckering in your work.

Embroidery stitches fall into two categories - those that are 'skimmed' (eg chain stitch, stem stitch, fly stitch and bullion knots) and those that are 'stabbed' (eg French knot, straight stitch, satin stitch, split stitch and couching).

Skimmed stitches are generally worked in one movement and from one side of the fabric. These stitches are best worked without a hoop so the fabric can be manipulated. Stabbed stitches are generally worked in two steps. The needle is taken to the back of the fabric and pulled through before returning to the front.

While some stitches can be either 'skimmed' or 'stabbed' (eg satin stitch), stabbing produces a better result. A hoop is a valuable aid when working stabbed stitches.

detached chain

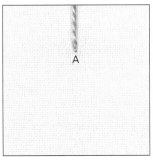

1. Secure the thread on the back of the fabric and bring it to the front at A. This is the base of the stitch.

2. Hold the thread to the left.

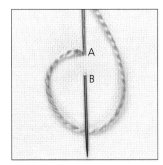

3. Take the needle to the back at A, through the same hole in the fabric. Re-emerge at B. Loop the thread under the tip of the needle.

4. Pull the thread through. The tighter you pull, the thinner the stitch will become.

5. To finish, take the needle to the back just over the end of the loop.

6. Pull the thread through and end off on the back of the fabric.

Did you know?

- Quilted petticoats were commonly worn by Dutch ladies during the eighteenth century. Because the men at the time also preferred stout women, many would wear between four and nine quilted petticoats at any one time.
- Hawaiians have developed a distinctive style of quilt incorporating appliqué. Originally introduced to the islands by New England missionaries in 1820, the Hawaiians developed symmetrical 'paper cut' style patterns inspired by their native flora and fauna.

encroaching stem stitch

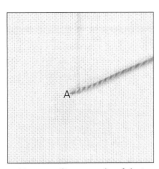

1. Draw a line on the fabric. Secure the thread on the back of the fabric and bring it to the front at A, on the lower end.

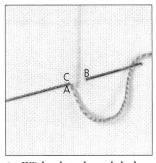

2. With the thread below the line, take the needle to the back at B and re-emerge at C. The needle is angled across the line.

3. Pull the thread through to complete the first stitch.

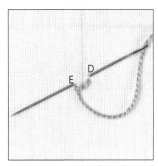

4. Again with the thread below the needle, take the needle to the back at D and re-emerge at E.

encroaching stem stitch / continued

5. Pull the thread through to complete the second stitch.

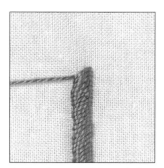

6. Continue working stitches in the same manner, always keeping the thread below the needle.

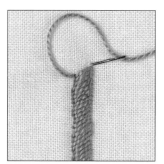

7. To finish, take the needle to the back for the last stitch but do not re-emerge.

8. Pull the thread through and end off on the back of the fabric.

feather stitch

1. Bring the thread to the front at A. This will be the left hand side of the stitch.

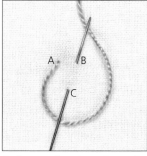

2. Loop the thread to the right and take the needle from B to C. Ensure the thread is under the tip of the needle.

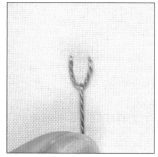

3. Pull the thread through in a downward movement and hold firmly with your thumb.

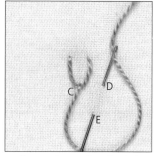

4. Again, loop the thread to the right and take the needle from D to E. Ensure the thread is under the tip of the needle.

5. Pull the thread through in the same manner as before.

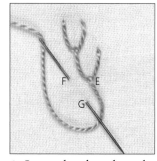

6. Loop the thread to the left and take the needle from F to G. Ensure the thread is under the tip of the needle.

7. Pull the thread through. Continue working stitches in the same manner.

8. To finish, take the needle to the back of the fabric just over the last loop. Pull the thread through and end off on the back of the fabric.

fly stitch

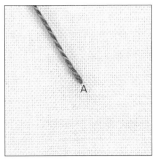
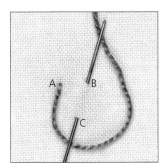

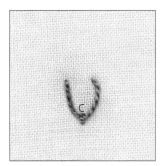

1. Secure the thread on the back of the fabric and bring it to the front at A. This will be the left hand side of the stitch.

2. Take the needle to the back at B and re-emerge at C. Loop the thread under the tip of the needle.

3. Hold the loop in place with your thumb (thumb not shown). Pull the thread until the loop lies snugly against C.

4. Take the thread to the back of the fabric below C to anchor the loop. End off the thread on the back of the fabric.

french knot

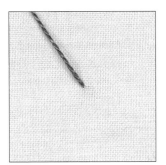

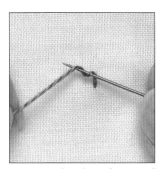

1. Secure the thread on the back of the fabric and bring it to the front at the position for the knot.

2. Hold the thread firmly approximately 3cm (1 1/8") from the fabric.

3. Take the thread over the needle, ensuring the needle points away from the fabric.

4. Wrap the thread around the needle. Keeping the thread taut, turn the tip of the needle towards the fabric.

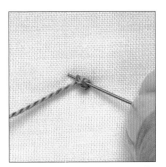

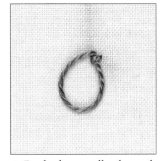
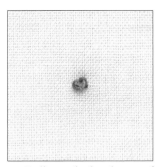

5. Take the tip of the needle to the back of the fabric approximately 1 - 2 fabric threads away from where it emerged.

6. Slide the knot down the needle onto the fabric. Pull the thread until the knot is firmly around the needle.

7. Push the needle through the fabric. Hold the knot in place with your thumb and pull the thread through (thumb not shown).

8. Pull until the loop of thread completely disappears. End off on the back of the fabric.

ghiordes knot

1. First row. Take the needle to the back at A. Pull the thread through, leaving a tail on the front of the fabric.

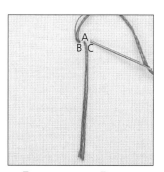

2. Re-emerge at B, just to the left of A. Take the needle to the back at C, just to the right of A.

3. Hold the tail taut and pull the thread through to form a straight stitch.

4. Re-emerge at A, behind the straight stitch.

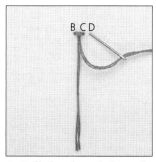

5. Pull the thread through. With the thread below the needle, take the needle to the back at D.

6. Pull the thread through, leaving a loop the same length as the tail.

7. Hold the loop in place with your thumb and bring the needle to the front at C (thumb not shown).

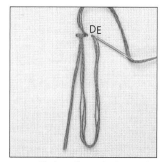

8. Pull the thread through. Take the needle to the back at E.

9. Pull the thread through to form a straight stitch. Bring the needle to the front at D, behind the straight stitch.

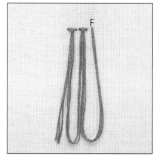

10. Pull the thread through. With the thread below the needle, take it to the back at F, leaving a loop on the front.

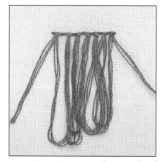

11. Continue to the end of the row in the same manner, finishing with the thread on the front. Ensure the last stitch is not a loop.

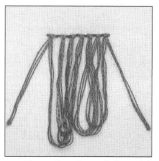

12. Trim the thread, leaving a tail the same length as the loops.

ghiordes knot / continued

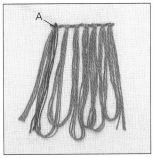

13. Second row. Take the needle to the back of the fabric directly above A. Pull the thread through, leaving a tail on the front of the fabric.

14. Work the second row in the same manner as the first row.

15. Continue working the required number of rows in the same manner. Stand the loops up and trim them evenly.

16. Alternate between combing and trimming until the stitches are the desired height and appearance.

granitos

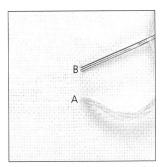

1. Secure the thread on the back of the fabric and bring it to the front at A. Pull the thread through and take it to the back at B.

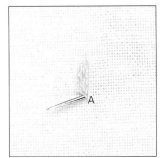

2. Pull the thread through. Re-emerge at A, taking care to come through exactly the same hole in the fabric as before.

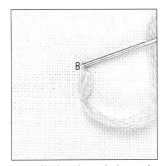

3. Pull the thread through. Take the needle to the back at B through exactly the same hole in the fabric as before.

4. Loop the thread to the left of the first stitch and begin to gently pull the thread through.

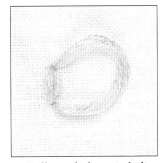

5. Pull until the stitch lies alongside the first stitch. Work a third stitch, looping the thread to the right of the first stitch.

6. Gently pull the thread through. Work the required number of stitches in the same manner, always alternating from side to side. Secure the thread on the back of the fabric.

The Embroidered Miniature Quilt by Helen Marshall

long and short stitch

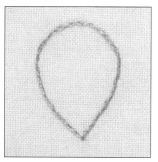

1. Draw the shape to be filled on the fabric. Outline the shape with your chosen stitch.

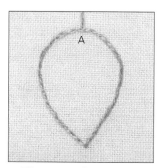

2. First row. Secure a new thread on the back of the fabric and bring it to the front at A, just outside the outline and near the centre.

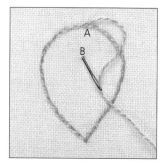

3. Take the needle to the back at B, within the shape.

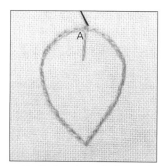

4. Pull the thread through. Re-emerge just beyond the outline, very close to A.

5. Pull the thread through. Work a second stitch that is slightly shorter than the first stitch.

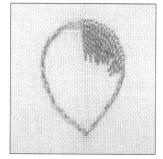

6. Continue working stitches very close together across one half of the shape. If necessary, fan them to fit the shape and alternate between long and short stitches.

7. Work across the remaining half in the same manner. End off the thread on the back of the fabric.

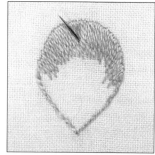

8. Second row. Bring the needle to the front, splitting a stitch of the previous row.

9. Pull the thread through. Take the needle to the back in the unembroidered area.

10. Pull the thread through to complete the first stitch.

11. Work stitches in the same direction as those in the first row. Always emerge through a previous stitch and keep all stitches the same length.

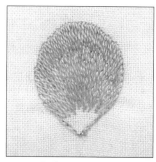

12. Subsequent rows. Continue working rows in the same manner as the second row.

Quilting in battle

As early as the 1300s, Mali warriors wore quilted suits of armor for protection in battle. In the Sudan, full quilted garments for both warriors and their horses were worn as protective armor in battle.

long and short stitch / continued

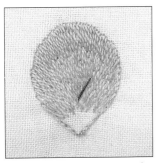

13. Last row. Bring the needle to the front, splitting a stitch of the previous row.

14. Pull the thread through. Take the needle to the back just over the outline.

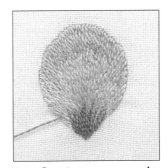

15. Continue across the row. Always emerge through a previous stitch, alternating between one long and one short stitch.

16. Complete the row, ensuring the outline is completely covered.

open fishbone stitch

1. Secure the thread on the back of the fabric and bring it to the front at A, on the left hand side near the top of the shape.

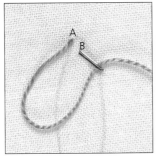

2. Take the needle to the back at B, diagonally below and to the right of the middle of the shape.

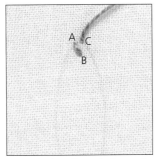

3. Pull the thread through. Re-emerge at C, on the right hand side directly opposite A. Pull the thread through.

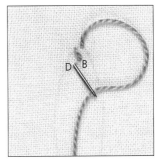

4. Take the needle to the back at D, just to the left and slightly below B. This stitch crosses the previous stitch.

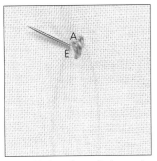

5. Pull the thread through. Re-emerge at E, a short distance below A.

6. Pull the thread through. Take the needle to the back at F. This stitch crosses the previous stitch.

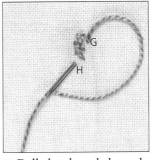

7. Pull the thread through. Re-emerge at G and take the needle to the back at H.

8. Continue working stitches in the same manner until the shape is filled. End off on the back of the fabric.

padded satin stitch

Single layer of padding

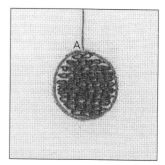

1. Draw the shape to be filled on the front of the fabric. Secure the thread on the back and outline the shape with your chosen stitch.

2. Bring the thread to the front just inside the outline. Work satin stitches across the shape, starting and ending each stitch just inside the outline.

3. Alternatively, work rows of chain stitch, starting and ending each row just inside the outline.

4. Secure a new thread on the back of the fabric. Bring it to the front at A, just outside the outline and near the centre.

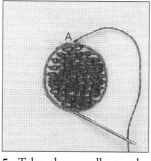

5. Take the needle to the back of the fabric on the opposite side of the shape and just outside the outline.

6. Pull the thread through and re-emerge on the opposite side, very close to A.

7. Pull the thread through. Continue working stitches in the same manner until the shape is completely covered.

8. To finish, take the needle to the back of the fabric after the last stitch. Pull the thread through and end off on the back of the fabric.

Multiple layers of padding

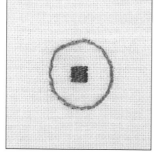

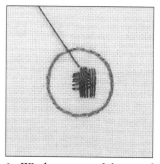

1. Draw the shape to be filled on the front of the fabric. Secure the thread on the back and outline the shape with your chosen stitch.

2. Work a layer of satin stitches in the middle of the shape.

3. Work a second layer of satin stitches, slightly larger than the first layer and in the opposite direction. Keep the stitches within the outline.

4. Work a final layer of satin stitches in the opposite direction to the previous layer, covering the outline.

pistil stitch

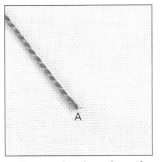

1. Secure the thread on the back of the fabric and bring it to the front at A, the base of the stitch.

2. Holding the thread firmly in the left hand, wrap the thread over the needle.

3. Keeping the thread taut, wrap it around the needle in a clockwise direction.

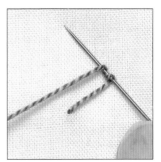

4. Still holding the thread taut, turn the needle towards the fabric.

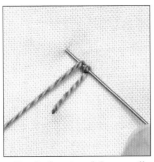

5. Push the tip of the needle through the fabric at the required position.

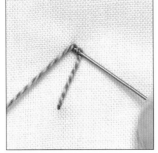

6. Keeping tension on the thread, slide the wraps down the needle onto the fabric.

7. Keeping your thumb over the wraps, begin to pull the thread through (thumb not shown).

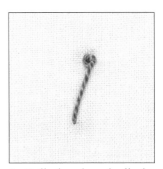

8. Pull the thread all the way through and end off on the back of the fabric.

running stitch

1. Mark a line on the fabric. Secure the thread on the back of the fabric and bring it to the front at the right hand end of the line.

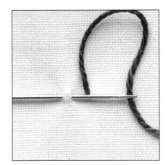

2. Take a small stitch, skimming the needle beneath the fabric along the line.

3. Pull the thread through. Take another stitch in the same manner as before, ensuring the stitch is the same length as the previous one.

4. Continue in the same manner to the end. Take the thread to the back of the fabric and end off.

satin stitch

1. Secure the thread on the back of the fabric. Work an outline around the shape using your chosen stitch.

2. Bring the thread to the front at A, just outside the outline and near the centre.

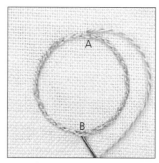

3. Take the needle to the back at B, just over the outline and directly opposite A.

4. Pull the thread through. Re-emerge next to A, angling the needle from under the outline.

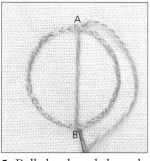

5. Pull the thread through. Take the needle to the back of the fabric next to B.

6. Pull the thread through to complete the second stitch.

7. Continue working stitches in the same manner. To finish, take the needle to the back of the fabric for the last stitch.

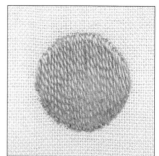

8. Pull the thread through and end off on the back of the fabric.

Hints for left handed embroiderers

For most stitches, work from right to left (or the opposite direction to right hander's instructions).

Most stitches are worked as a mirror image to the way right handers work them. When following instructions, imagine you are looking into a mirror rather than copying exactly what you see.

Some instructions will be easier to follow if you turn them upside down.

When wrapping, twisting or looping thread, do it in the same direction as in the instructions for right handers.

Stitches that are worked from top to bottom for right handers are also worked from top to bottom for left handers and vice versa.

scroll stitch

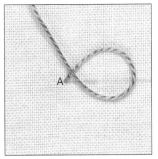

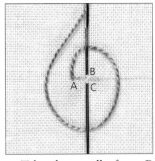

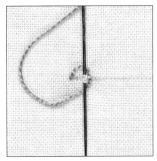

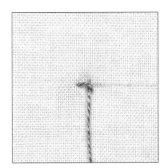

1. Secure the thread on the back of the fabric and bring it to the front at A on the left hand side. Make a loop to the right of A in a clockwise direction.

2. Take the needle from B to C, taking a tiny stitch on the marked line. Ensure the circle of thread lies under both ends of the needle.

3. Pull the thread firmly until the loop tightens around the needle.

4. Pull the needle and thread through in a downward direction.

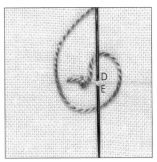

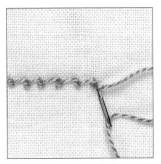

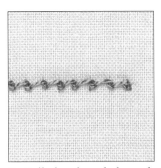

5. Loop the thread in a clockwise direction to the right of the scroll.

6. Take the needle from D to E, taking a tiny stitch on the marked line as before. Ensure the circle of thread lies under both ends of the needle.

7. Pull the thread through. Continue working stitches across the row in the same manner. To end off, take the needle to the back just below the scroll of the last stitch.

8. Pull the thread through and end off on the back of the fabric.

Threading needles

Ensure that the end of the thread has been cut cleanly. Any stray fibres can push the thread away from the needle when you try to thread it.

Moisten the end of the thread and flatten it between your fingers. After threading, cut the moist piece off.

Ensure you are threading with the grain running down the thread. If you are using the wrong end, it can 'frizz up' as you try to push it through the eye.

When threading wools, try folding the end of the yarn around the needle. Pinch it tightly and slide it off the needle. Push the folded piece through the eye.

If you have real difficulty, try a needle that is a size larger.

seed stitch

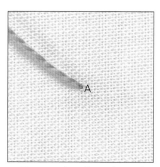

1. Secure the thread on the back of the fabric and bring it to the front at A.

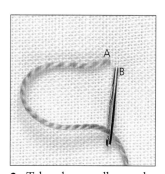

2. Take the needle to the back at B, a very short distance away.

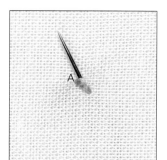

3. Pull the thread through and re-emerge next to A.

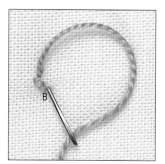

4. Pull the thread through. Take the needle to the back next to B.

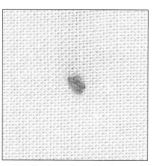

5. Pull the thread through to complete the stitch.

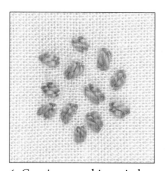

6. Continue working stitches in the same manner, scattering them within the area to be filled and varying the angle of the stitches.

Storing your quilt

- The ideal storage place for a quilt is on an unused bed. Lay it out flat over the mattress pad, layering the quilts if you have several. Cover with a clean sheet to prevent dust and exposure to light.
- An alternative method of storing a quilt is to roll it on a cardboard tube or plastic pipe. Be sure to cover the plastic or cardboard with layers of clean muslin or acid-free paper. Cover the quilt again with another sheet or more acid-free tissue.

split stitch

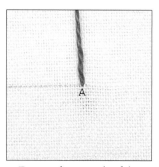

1. Draw a line on the fabric. Secure the thread on the back of the fabric and bring it to the front at A, on the right hand end.

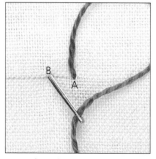

2. Take the needle to the back at B, a short distance away.

3. Pull the thread through. Bring the needle to the front at C, splitting the thread in the middle of the first stitch.

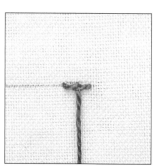

4. Pull the thread through.

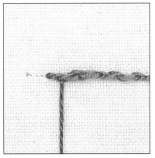

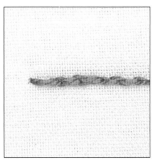

5. Take the needle to the back at D. C - D is the same distance as A - B.

6. Pull the thread through. Bring the needle to the front at B, splitting the thread in the middle of the second stitch.

7. Pull the thread through. Continue working stitches in the same manner.

8. Pull the thread through and end off on the back of the fabric.

stem stitch

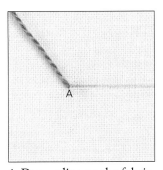

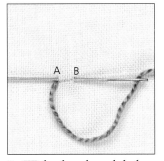

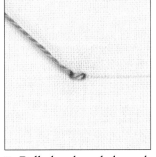

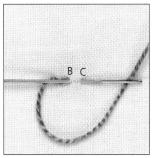

1. Draw a line on the fabric. Secure the thread on the back of the fabric and bring it to the front at A, on the left hand end.

2. With the thread below the needle, take the needle to the back at B and re-emerge at A.

3. Pull the thread through to complete the first stitch.

4. Again with the thread below the needle, take the needle to the back at C and re-emerge at B.

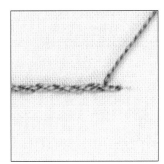

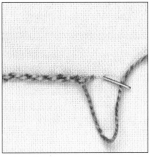

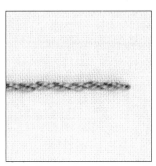

5. Pull the thread through to complete the second stitch.

6. Continue working stitches in the same manner, always keeping the thread below the needle.

7. To finish, take the needle to the back for the last stitch but do not re-emerge.

8. Pull the thread through and end off on the back of the fabric.

straight stitch

   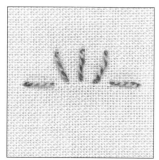

1. Secure the thread on the back of the fabric and bring it to the front at A.

2. Take the needle to the back at B.

3. Pull the thread through. Secure the thread on the back of the fabric.

4. Several straight stitches worked together.

whipped stem stitch

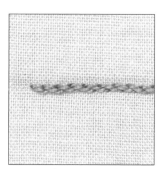 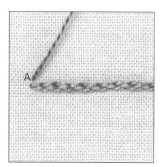 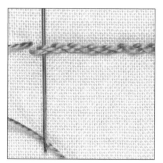 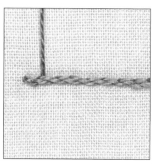

1. Foundation. Work a line of stem stitch following the instructions on page 109.

2. Whipping. Secure the thread on the back of the fabric and bring it to the front at A, just above the first stem stitch.

3. Slide the needle from bottom to top under the space shared by the first and second stem stitches. Do not go through the fabric.

4. Pull the thread through.

 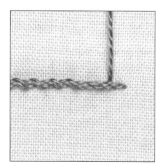  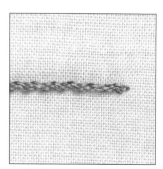

5. Slide the needle from bottom to top under the space shared by the second and third stem stitches. Do not go through the fabric.

6. Pull the thread through. Continue to the end of the stem stitch in the same manner.

7. To finish, take the needle to the back of the fabric behind the last stem stitch.

8. Pull the thread through and end off on the back of the fabric.

straight seam

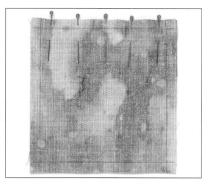

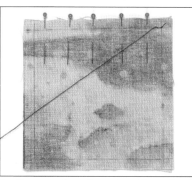

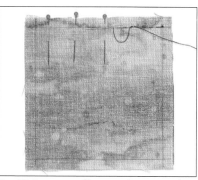

1. Mark the stitchline around the outer edge of each piece. Place two pieces right sides together, carefully matching the marked stitchlines. Placing pins at right angles to the stitchline, pin the pieces together at 2.5cm (1") intervals and exactly at the marked corners.

2. Secure the thread with a back stitch exactly at the marked corner. (The corner on the right hand side for right handers and the corner on the left hand side for left handers.)

3. Using small running stitches (approximately 8 stitches to the inch or 2.5cm), begin stitching along the marked stitchline.

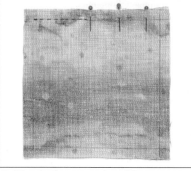

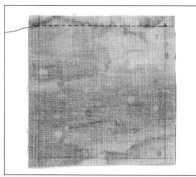

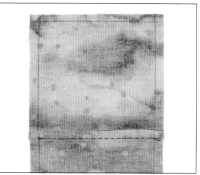

4. Check the opposite side to ensure the stitches go through both marked stitchlines. If they do not, remove the stitches and re-align the stitch lines.

5. Removing the pins as you go, stitch to the end of the marked stitchline.

6. Secure the thread with a back stitch and trim. Press.

butted seam

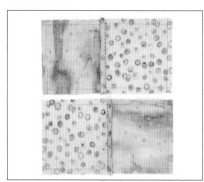

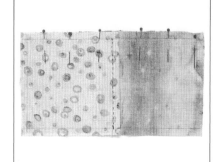

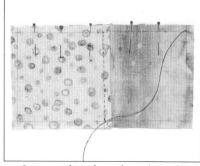

1. Make two pairs of seamed pieces following the instructions above. Open out each pair and press the seams to one side.

2. Place the two pairs, right sides together, carefully matching the marked stitchlines and butted seams. Placing pins at right angles to the stitchline, pin the pieces together at 2.5cm (1") intervals and exactly at the marked corners and butted seam.

3. Secure the thread with a back stitch exactly at the marked corner. (The corner on the right hand side for right handers and the corner on the left hand side for left handers.)

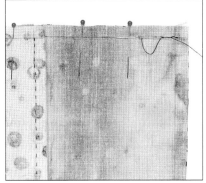

4. Using small running stitches (approximately 8 stitches to the inch or 2.5cm), begin stitching along the marked stitchline.

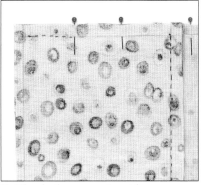

5. Check the opposite side to ensure the stitches go through both marked stitchlines. If they do not, remove the stitches and re-align the stitchlines.

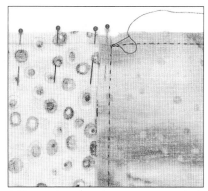

6. Removing the pins as you go, stitch to the pin at the butted seam. Do not stitch through the seam allowance, push it out of the way towards the unstitched section.

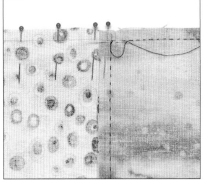

7. Remove the pin. Work a back stitch at the marked corner next to the butted seam.

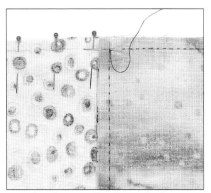

8. Take the needle through the seam allowance only.

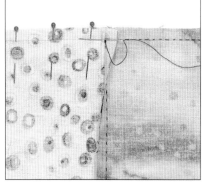

9. Pull the thread through. Push the seam allowance back towards the previous stitching. Work a back stitch at the marked corner.

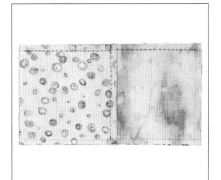

10. Removing the pins as you go, stitch to the end of the marked stitchline. Secure the thread with a back stitch and trim.

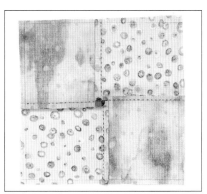

11. Press the seams as shown.

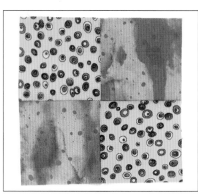

12. Right side of fabric.

set in seam

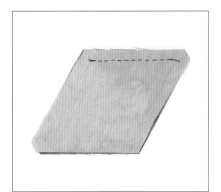

1. Pin and stitch two pieces together following the instructions for a straight seam on page 112.

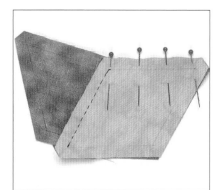

2. With right sides together and carefully matching the marked stitchlines, place a third piece onto the first piece. Placing pins at right angles to the stitchline, pin the pieces together at 2.5cm (1") intervals and exactly at the marked corners.

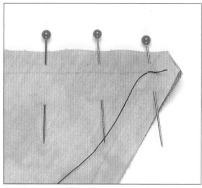

3. Secure the thread with a back stitch exactly at the marked corner. (The corner on the right hand side for right handers and the corner on the left hand side for left handers.)

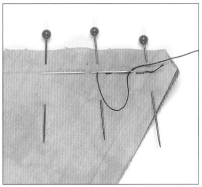

4. Using small running stitches (approximately 8 stitches to the inch or 2.5cm), begin stitching along the marked stitchline.

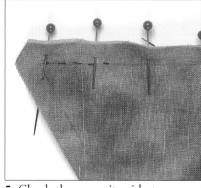

5. Check the opposite side to ensure the stitches go through both marked stitchlines. If they do not, remove the stitches and re-align the stitchlines.

6. Removing the pins as you go, stitch to the pin at the corner. Ensure the seam allowance on the first piece is out of the way.

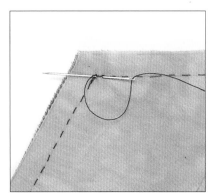

7. Remove the pin. Work a back stitch at the marked corner next to the end of the previous seam.

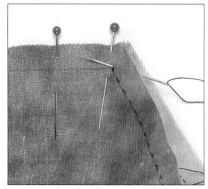

8. Pivot the third piece at the corner and pin the adjacent side to the second piece. Ensure the stitchlines match. Take the needle through the seam allowance only.

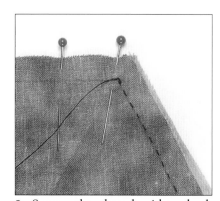

9. Secure the thread with a back stitch exactly at the marked corner.

10. Stitch along this side in the same manner as before, finishing with a back stitch at the corner.

11. Press the seams flat.

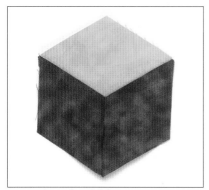

12. Right side of fabric.

PIECING BY MACHINE

straight seam

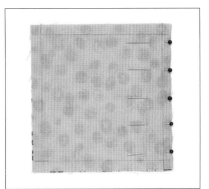

1. Place two pieces right sides together, carefully matching raw edges. Placing pins at right angles to the stitchline, pin the pieces together.

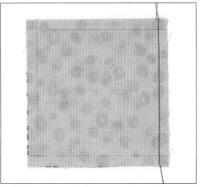

2. Using a machine straight stitch and leaving a 6mm (1/4") seam allowance, stitch from edge to edge.

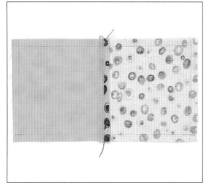

3. Press the seam open.

Sizes of quilts

Comforter - the quilt lies on the top of a mattress with no overhang and pillows are placed on top of the quilt.

Coverlet - the quilt covers the sides of the mattress and the pillows.

Bedspread - the quilt reaches almost to the floor and covers the pillows.

If you have a specific bed in mind, measure this bed as mattress sizes can vary. For a quilt that is to be used as a coverlet or bedspread, add approximately 30cm (12") to the length of the mattress and overhang at the end to ensure the quilt will adequately cover the pillows and be able to tuck under them.

chain piecing

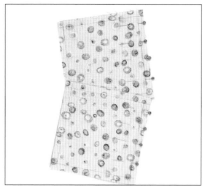

1. Pin pairs of pieces together, following step 1 on page 115.

2. Stitch along one side of the first pinned pair, following step 2 on page 115. Take 2 - 3 more stitches beyond the edge of the pieces.

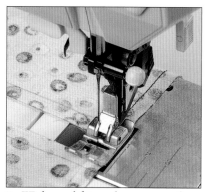

3. Without lifting the presser foot, begin to feed a second pinned pair under the foot.

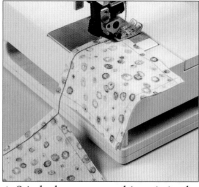

4. Stitch the seam on this pair in the same manner as before. Take 2 - 3 more stitches beyond the edge of the pieces.

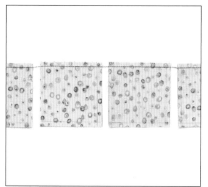

5. Continue stitching pieces in the same manner until the desired number are complete.

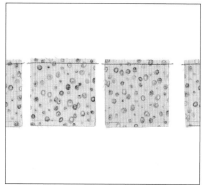

6. Cut the stitching between the pairs to separate them.

butted seam

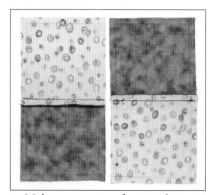

1. Make two pairs of seamed pieces following the instructions on page 115. Press the seams flat.

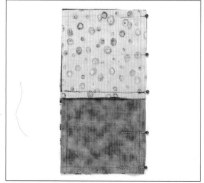

2. With right sides together and matching raw edges and seams, pin the two seamed pieces together. Ensure the pins are at right angles to the stitchline and the seam allowances face in opposite directions.

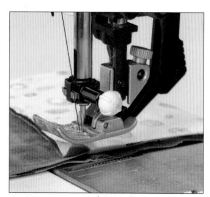

3. Using a machine straight stitch, stitch up to the butted seams. Finish with the needle in the down position. Lift the presser foot and recheck that the seams are aligned.

butted seam

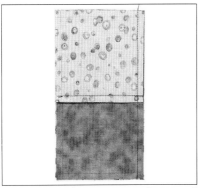

4. Lower the presser foot and continue stitching to the end.

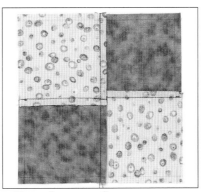

5. Press the seams flat.

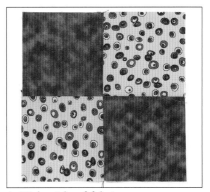

6. Right side of fabric.

set in seam

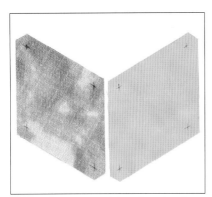

1. On the wrong side of each piece, mark the seam allowances at the corners.

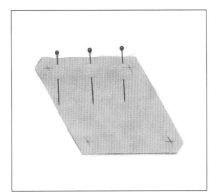

2. Place two pieces right sides together, ensuring the markings are aligned. Pin, placing the pins at right angles to the stitchline.

3. Starting and finishing at the marked corners, and securing the thread at the beginning and end, stitch the seam with a machine straight stitch.

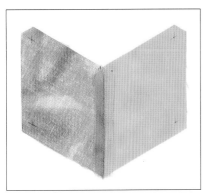

4. Press the seam open.

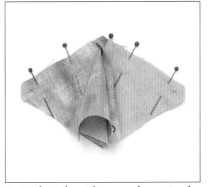

5. With right sides together, pin the third piece to the first two pieces in the same manner as in step 2.

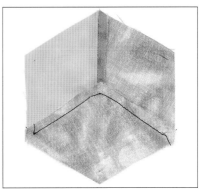

6. Stitch from corner mark to corner mark, pivoting at the seam. Press.

blocking

No matter how meticulous you are, it is very rare for pieced blocks to turn out flat or even identical.
For best results, each block needs to be blocked before assembling the quilt top.

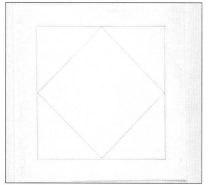

1. Transfer the full size pattern for the block to a piece of paper.

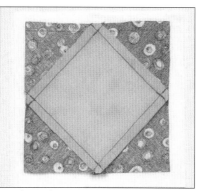

2. Place the paper pattern onto your ironing board or similar padded surface. Place the block face down over the paper pattern.

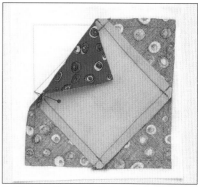

3. Using fine small headed pins (eg silk pins) and starting from the centre, take a pin through a seam or corner. Push it through the corresponding place on the paper pattern and then into the padded surface.

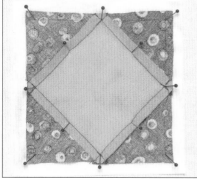

4. Continue pinning in this manner, slightly stretching or easing the block to fit the pattern.

5. When the block is completely pinned out, apply steam to the entire piece by holding a steam iron just above the fabric and slowly moving it about. Do not press.

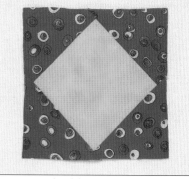

6. Leave the block to cool and dry completely. Remove the pins and handle gently until it is sewn into the quilt top.

Laundering quilts

The gentlest way to clean a quilt is to vacuum it. Do this at least every six months. Lay the quilt out flat and vacuum both sides using a soft upholstery nozzle.

For a pure cotton quilt, gently hand wash it in your bathtub using a very mild soap powder or liquid. Rinse the quilt thoroughly and roll it in towelling to remove as much water as possible. Lay it out flat to dry.

Drycleaning is the most appropriate method to use for quilts made from silk and wool. Ensure your chosen cleaner is experienced with this type of work before committing your precious quilt to their care.

If your quilt has been made with machine washable fabrics, machine wash it using the gentlest settings on your machine. Dry in the same manner as a hand washed quilt.

setting blocks together

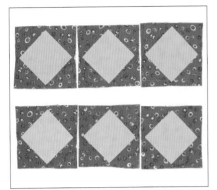

1. Lay out the blocks and check that they are correctly positioned.

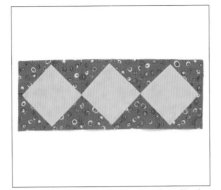

2. Hand or machine stitch all the blocks in the first row together to form a strip.

3. Repeat for the remaining rows.

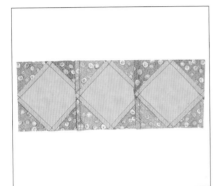

4. Press all the seams of the first row in the same direction.

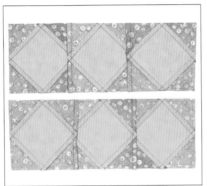

5. Press all the seams of the second row in the opposite direction to those of the first row. Repeat for the remaining rows, alternating the direction from row to row.

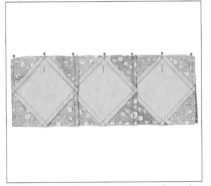

6. Place the first two rows right sides together. Pin the ends and then pin the seams together, ensuring they are accurately aligned.

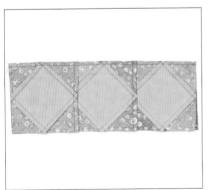

7. Hand or machine stitch the two rows together. Press.

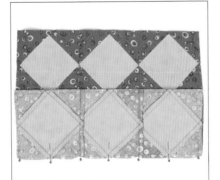

8. With right sides together, pin the top of the third row to the lower edge of the second row in the same manner as before.

9. Stitch and press. Continue attaching the remaining rows in the same manner.

sashing

Sashing creates a framework around each block and is a common alternative to simply setting the blocks together. As a guide, the finished sashing should be approximately one quarter the width of the finished blocks.

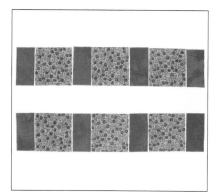

1. Lay out the blocks and check that they are correctly positioned. Cut sashing strips the same height as the blocks and place them between the blocks in each row.

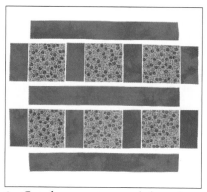

2. Cut long strips and lay them between the rows.

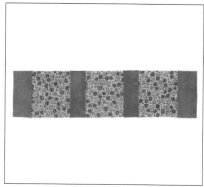

3. Hand or machine stitch all the blocks and strips in the first row together to form a long strip.

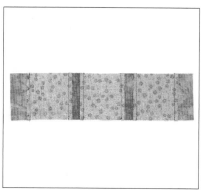

4. Press all the seam allowances towards the sashing.

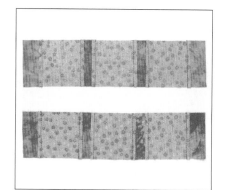

5. Stitch and press the blocks and sashing pieces for the remaining rows in the same manner.

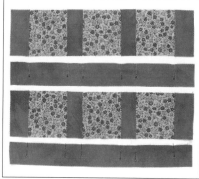

6. Mark the long strips with pins at the positions that align with the block seams.

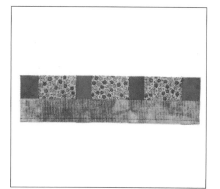

7. With right sides together and matching markings with seams, pin one long strip to a row of blocks. Stitch.

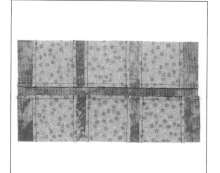

8. Pin and stitch a row of blocks to the other edge of the strip. Press the seam allowances towards the sashing.

9. Continue attaching the remaining strips in the same manner.

measuring for borders

To ensure your quilt will lie flat and be a proper square or rectangle, it is important to measure border pieces accurately. Borders on opposite sides need to be exactly the same length.

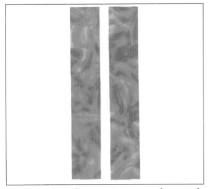

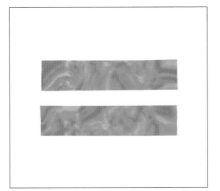

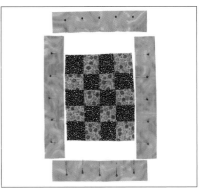

1. Side borders. Measure the quilt top along both sides and down the centre. Add the three measurements together and divide by three. Cut the side borders to this measurement plus enough to finish the corners by your chosen method.

2. Upper and lower borders. Measure the quilt top along the upper and lower edges and across the centre. Calculate the measurement as in step 1. Cut the end borders to this measurement plus enough to finish the corners by your chosen method.

3. Place a pin at each end of one side border to mark the same measurement as the side of the quilt top (the measurement from step 1). Aligning pins, fold the border into quarters and mark each fold with a pin. Repeat for the remaining pieces.

borders with butted corners

Cut side borders to measure the same length as the sides of the quilt top. Cut the upper and lower borders to measure the same as the end of the quilt top plus twice the border strip width, less 2.5cm (1").

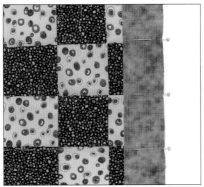

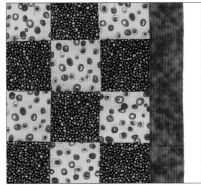

1. Mark the sides and ends of the quilt top with pins at the quarter and halfway points. Ensure the border strips are marked in the same manner (see above).

2. With right sides together and matching pins, pin one side border to one side of the quilt top. Slightly stretch or ease the border as necessary.

3. Hand or machine stitch the border to the quilt top. Press the seam towards the border.

Fact or Fiction?

Before electricity women typically quilted in the evening by the fireside.

It was and still is difficult to do fine stitching in poor light. Before modern lighting was available most quilting was done in the daylight, outside if possible. A good deal of quilting was done in the summer due to longer daylight hours. Farm women may have been too busy to quilt during planting and harvest time but they quilted when they could find the time in the lighter months.

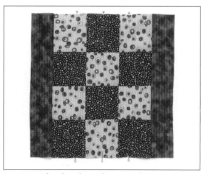

4. Attach the border to the opposite side of the quilt top in the same manner and press as before.

5. Pin and stitch the upper border in the same manner as the side borders, ensuring the ends line up with the outer edges of the side borders. Press as before.

6. Attach the border to the opposite end of the quilt top in the same manner and press as before.

borders with mitred corners

Cut side borders to measure the same length as the sides of the quilt top, plus twice the border width, plus 5cm (2"). Cut upper and lower borders to measure the same length as the ends of the quilt top, plus twice the border width, plus 5cm (2").

1. Mark the sides and ends of the quilt top with pins at the quarter and halfway points. Ensure the border strips are marked in the same manner (see page 121).

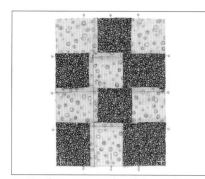

2. On the wrong side of the quilt top, mark the position at each corner where the stitchlines cross.

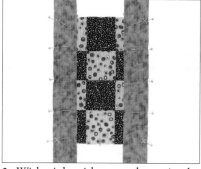

3. With right sides together, pin the side borders to the quilt top. Transfer the marked corner spots to the borders by pushing a pin through at each mark and marking the border where the pin emerges.

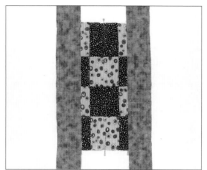

4. Starting and finishing at the marked spots, stitch the side borders in place.

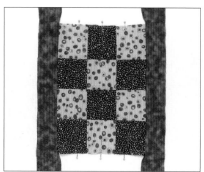

5. Press the seam allowances towards the borders.

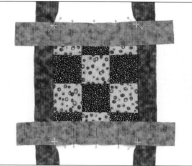

6. Pin the upper and lower border pieces to the quilt top and mark the corner spots in the same manner as before.

borders with mitred corners / continued

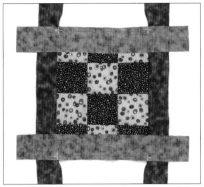

7. Keeping the side borders out of the way and starting and finishing at the marked spots, stitch the upper and lower borders in place.

8. Press the seam allowances towards the borders.

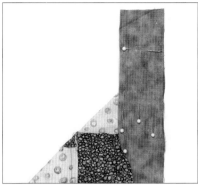

9. With right sides together, fold the quilt top in half diagonally. At one corner, temporarily fold the border seam allowances towards the quilt top and align the inner edges of the border pieces. Pin together.

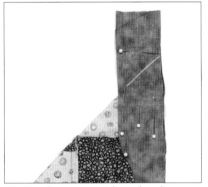

10. On the wrong side, rule a line at a 45° angle from the end of the stitching to the opposite side of the border.

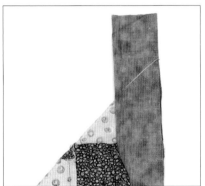

11. Starting exactly at the end of the previous stitching, stitch along the ruled line.

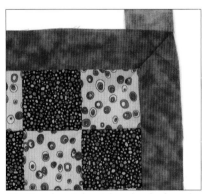

12. On the right side, check that the mitre will lay flat.

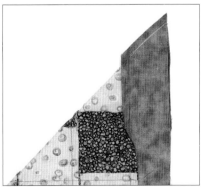

13. Trim the seam allowance to 6mm (¹/₄").

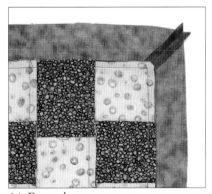

14. Press the seam open.

15. Form a mitre at the three remaining corners in the same manner.

borders with cornerstones

Cut side borders to measure the same length as the sides of the quilt top. Cut end borders to measure the same as the ends of the quilt top. Cut four corner squares the same size as the width of the border pieces.

1. Attach the side borders following steps 1 - 4 of butted corners on pages 121 - 122.

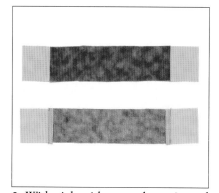

2. With right sides together, pin and stitch a corner square to each end of the upper and lower border pieces. Press the seam allowances away from the squares.

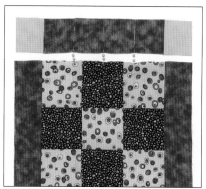

3. Mark the ends of the quilt top with pins at the quarter and halfway points. Ensure the border strips are marked in the same manner (see page 121).

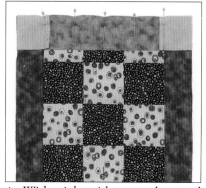

4. With right sides together and matching marks and seams, pin the upper border to the upper edge of the quilt top.

5. Stitch. Press the seam allowances towards the border.

6. Attach the remaining border piece in the same manner.

Sashing and borders

Plan borders at the initial design stages of your quilt. Borders added as an afterthought tend to either dominate or dilute the overall effect of the design.

Ensure the quilt top is well pressed and squared before measuring for the border pieces.

If using a fabric that is printed off-grain, cut the pieces following the print rather than the grain of the fabric.

Cut the longest border pieces first. This way you are less likely to run out of fabric.

Use a metal tape measure to measure your quilt as there is less likely to be any room for error and double check measurements before cutting your fabric.

Cut strips with a rotary cutter rather than scissors. It is easier to achieve a perfectly straight edge.

If the border is made up of multiple strips of fabric, sew the strips together before making mitred corners.

If you are not using sashing, press the seams of alternate rows of blocks in opposite directions.

preparing the lining

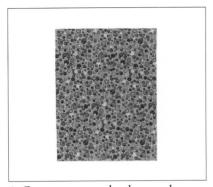

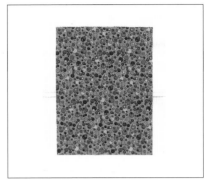

1. Cut away any selvedges and press. Cut out the lining to the size of the quilt top plus 10cm (4") longer and wider.

2. Alternatively, cut lengths of fabric and sew together. Press the seams open.

3. Cut out the lining to the measurements in step 1.

layering

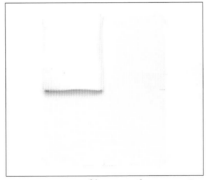

1. Spread the lining out flat, face down onto a large flat surface (eg floor or large table). Hold in place with masking tape. Mark the centre of each side.

2. Cut a piece of batting the same size as the lining. Fold into quarters. Position onto one quarter of the lining. Align the edges and folds of the batting with the edges and centre marks of the lining.

3. Gently unfold the batting, taking care not to stretch it. Carefully smooth out any wrinkles.

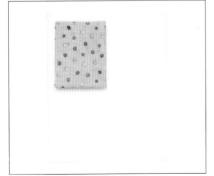

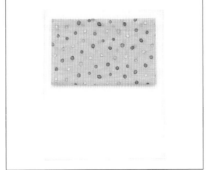

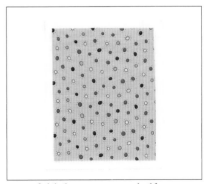

4. With the right side to the inside, fold the quilt top in quarters. Position it onto one quarter of the batting, aligning the folds with the centre marks. The raw edges of the quilt top should be an even 5cm (2") inside the batting.

5. Gently unfold the quilt top to cover half of the batting. The wrong side should be uppermost, with all cut edges 5cm (2") inside the batting.

6. Unfold the remaining half.

basting with pins

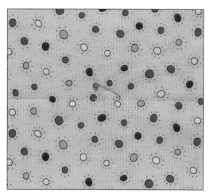

1. Beginning at the centre, take a safety pin through all three layers. Do not close the safety pin.

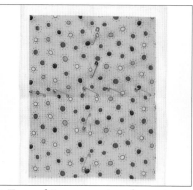

2. From this centre pin, place pins at regular intervals out to one side and end of the quilt along the centre lines. Place the pins approximately 8cm - 10cm (3" - 4") apart.

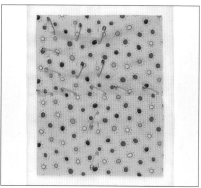

3. Smoothing the quilt top as you go, continue placing pins in one quarter of the quilt. Avoid pinning exactly on any marked quilting lines.

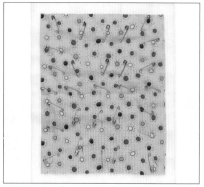

4. Pin the three remaining quarters in the same manner.

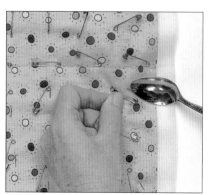

5. Close all the pins. Using a teaspoon can make this easier. Slide the bowl under the tip of the pin and twist slightly to lift the tip and catch it.

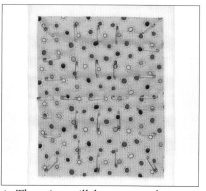

6. The pins will be removed as you quilt.

Hints on basting

Store your safety pins, open, in a lidded box.
This will save you considerable time on your next quilt.
A full size quilt will require approximately 500 pins!

Keep pins sharp by inserting the tips into an emery strawberry.
Push the pin into the strawberry, hold the strawberry firmly to compress the emery inside, then rotate the pin to sharpen it.

When basting with thread, use a light coloured thread that contrasts with your quilt. Dark coloured threads may permanently mark the quilt.

Make your basting stitches approximately 5cm (2") long on the top of the quilt and 12mm ($^1/_2$") long on the underside.

basting with thread

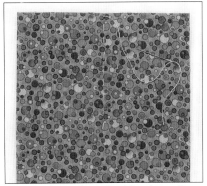

1. Use a long thread with a large knot in the end and a long needle (eg darning needle). Beginning at the centre, work long running stitches to the top of the quilt.

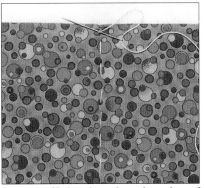

2. End off the thread at the edge of the quilt top with two small back stitches.

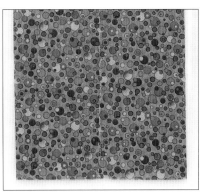

3. Again beginning from the centre, stitch to the lower edge and end off the thread in the same manner.

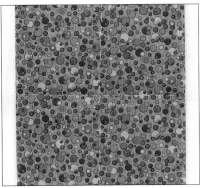

4. Repeat the procedure, stitching from the centre to one side of the quilt and then from the centre to the opposite side.

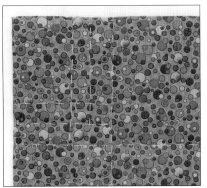

5. Starting near the centre basting each time, begin to fill in one quarter of the quilt with a grid of stitching lines approximately 8cm - 10cm (3" - 4") apart.

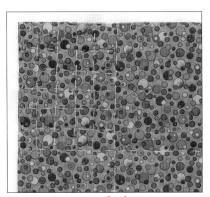

6. Continue until the quarter is completely covered.

7. Work the remaining quarters in the same manner.

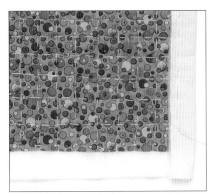

8. Fold the excess batting and lining on one edge onto the right side of the quilt top. Tack in place.

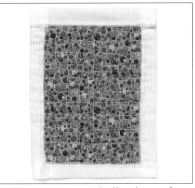

9. Continue around all sides to form a temporary binding. This will help prevent the edges from fraying as you quilt.

knotting the thread

This method creates a knot just the right size for quilting.

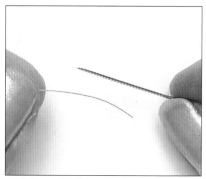 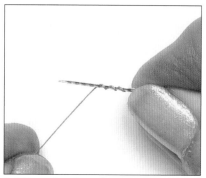 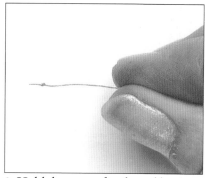

1. Thread the needle. Hold the thread against the tip of the needle approximately 2.5cm (1") from the end.

2. Wrap the thread around the tip of the needle three times.

3. Hold the wraps firmly and begin to pull the needle through. Pull until a knot forms near the end of the thread.

starting the thread

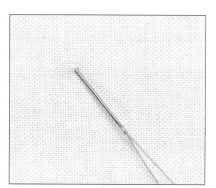 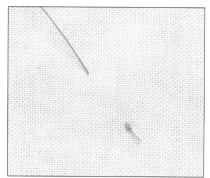 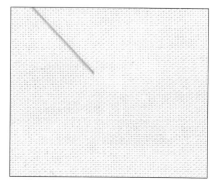

1. Beginning on the right side, insert the needle into the quilt top approximately 15mm (5/8") away from the starting point.

2. Take the needle into the batting only. Re-emerge at the starting position. Pull the thread until the knot lies on the surface of the fabric.

3. Gently tug the thread to sink the knot beneath the surface into the batting.

ending off the thread

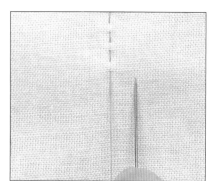 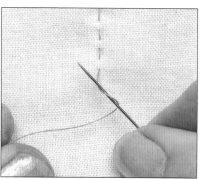 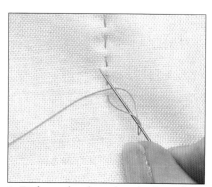

1. Pull the thread taut towards you. Hold the needle on the right hand side of the thread so it points towards the fabric.

2. Take the needle over and then under the thread to form a wrap around the needle.

3. Pick up the thread and take it from right to left behind the tip of the needle. The thread around the needle will resemble a figure eight.

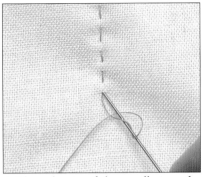

4. Place the tip of the needle into the fabric through exactly the same hole from which it last emerged.

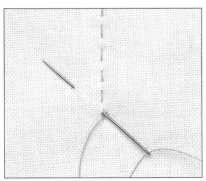

5. Take the needle into the batting and re-emerge through the quilt top a short distance away.

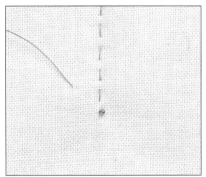

6. Pull the thread taut so the knot lies on the surface.

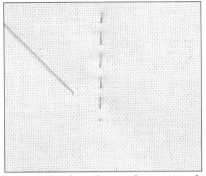

7. Give the thread a gentle tug to sink the knot beneath the surface.

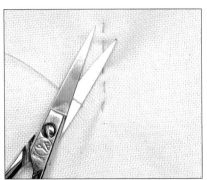

8. Pull the thread firmly to slightly pucker the fabric. Cut the thread close to the fabric.

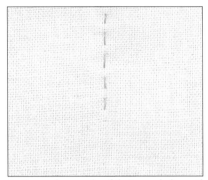

9. Smooth out the fabric and the tail will disappear beneath the surface.

quilting without a hoop or frame

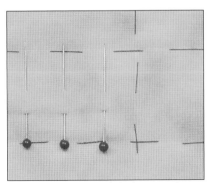

1. Place one hand below and one above the quilt and smooth the fabric along the line to be quilted. Pinning through all layers, place several pins across this line.

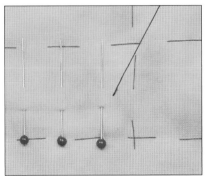

2. Secure the thread following the instructions on page 128.

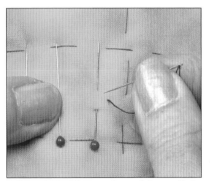

3. Firmly hold a section of the quilt in one hand with fingers below and thumb on top. Hold the needle so it lies above your hand rather than below (a bit like holding a pen).

quilting without a hoop or frame / continued

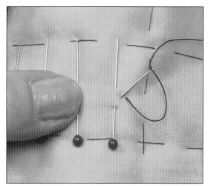

4. Push the needle through all layers until approximately half the needle extends from the back.

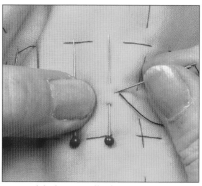

5. Hold the needle horizontally. Pull it backwards and run the tip along the lining fabric with your fingers following until it is at the spot you want to bring it to the front.

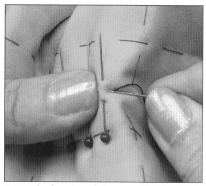

6. Push the tip of the needle upwards with your fingers, applying pressure from the top with your thumb, until the tip is as close as possible to 90° to the fabric.

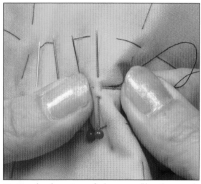

7. Push the tip of the needle through the quilt.

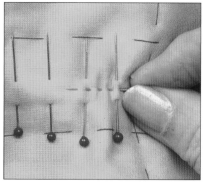

8. Repeat steps 4 - 7, putting as many stitches on the needle as you can comfortably manage.

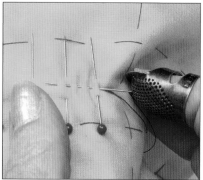

9. Push the needle through with your middle finger.

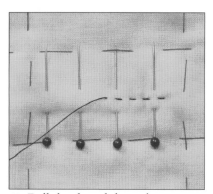

10. Pull the thread through.

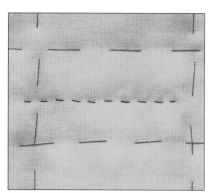

11. Continue repeating steps 4 - 10 for the entire line of quilting.

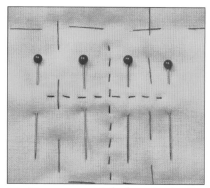

12. Repeat step 1 before beginning each new line of quilting unless other lines of quilting already stabilize the layers of fabric.

quilting in a hoop or frame

While you don't always have a choice, it is best to quilt towards yourself wherever possible.
Before you start, secure the thread following the instructions on page 128.

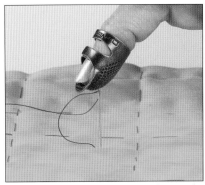

1. With one hand below the quilt, balance the needle at a 90° angle on the top of the quilt. Do not push it through.

2. Gently guiding and rocking the needle with your middle finger only, push it through until you just feel the tip on the underside.

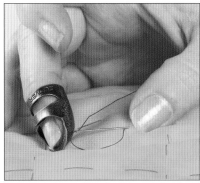

3. Lay the needle all the way back so the tip is pointing upwards. Push upwards with the finger below the quilt while pushing downwards with your thumb at the position immediately in front of the tip of the needle.

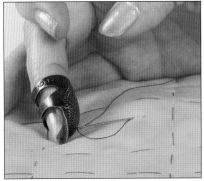

4. Reapply pressure to the end of the needle with your middle finger to force it back up to the surface. Stop pushing as soon as the tip of the needle is visible.

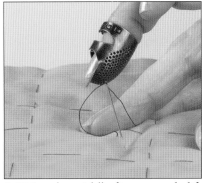

5. Using the middle finger, gently lift the needle until it is at a 90° angle to the top of the quilt and you can barely feel the tip on the underside.

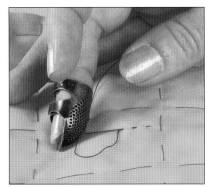

6. Repeat steps 1 - 5 to place a second stitch on the needle.

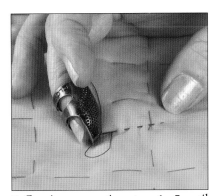

7. Continue repeating steps 1 - 5 until you cannot return the needle to a 90° angle to the top of the quilt.

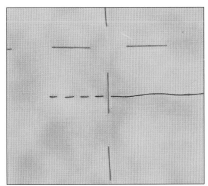

8. Pull the thread through.

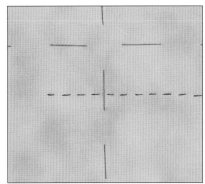

9. Continue repeating steps 1 - 8 for the entire line of quilting.

starting and finishing

The threads need to be locked in position at the beginning and end of each line of stitching.
This prevents them unravelling at a later date and also ensures that your stitching starts
and ends exactly where you want it to.

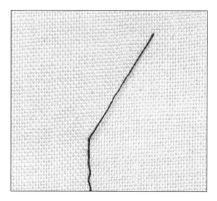

Method 1

1. Place the quilt under the presser foot and lower the needle into the fabric at the position where you wish to start stitching.

2. Set the stitch length to 0. Work several stitches, finishing with the needle in the down position.

3. Adjust the stitch length to the desired length of your quilting stitch and continue stitching.

4. Repeat step 2 to secure the thread at the end of the line.

5. Trim the tails of thread to approximately 2.5cm (1").

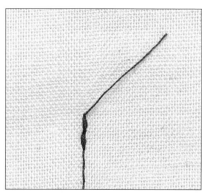

Method 2

1. Place the quilt under the presser foot and lower the needle into the fabric at the position where you wish to start stitching.

2. Use the securing function built into your sewing machine (if available).

3. Continue stitching.

4. Repeat step 2 to secure the thread at the end of the line.

5. Trim the tails of thread to approximately 2.5cm (1").

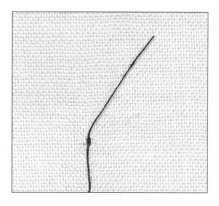

Method 3

1. Place the quilt under the presser foot and lower the needle into the fabric at the position where you wish to start stitching.

2. Set the stitch length to the desired length for your quilting stitch. As you begin to stitch, hold the fabric firmly so it cannot move for the first few stitches.

3. Release the pressure on the fabric and continue stitching.

4. Repeat step 2 to secure the thread at the end of the line.

5. Trim the tails of thread to approximately 2.5cm (1").

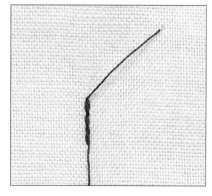

Method 4

1. Place the quilt under the presser foot and lower the needle into the fabric at the position where you wish to start stitching.

2. Set the stitch length to the desired length for your quilting stitch. Work forward for approximately three stitches.

3. Stitch in reverse back to the beginning and then stitch forward.

4. Reverse the procedure to secure the thread at the end of the line.

5. Trim the tails of thread to approximately 2.5cm (1").

trimming the tails of thread

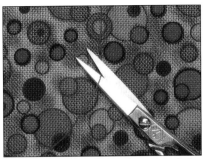

1. Cut the thread on the top of the quilt as close as possible to the fabric.

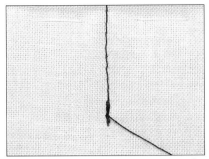

2. Turn the quilt over. Give the bobbin thread a gentle tug to pull the end of the top thread into the batting.

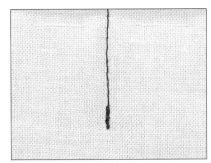

3. Cut the bobbin thread as close as possible to the fabric.

quilting with the feed dog engaged

This method is suitable for stitching in straight lines or gentle curves.
Always work the longest stitch lines first and then fill in any shorter ones.

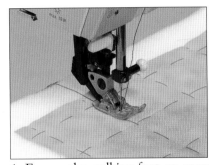

1. Engage the walking foot on your machine and set the stitch length to 2.5. Lock the threads at the beginning of the stitchline using your chosen method (see previous page).

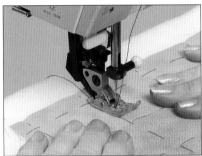

2. As you stitch, hold the fabric on either side, and just in front of the presser foot with both hands to keep it smooth.

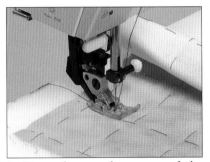

3. To work near the centre of the quilt, feed the quilt from left to right under the raised presser foot. Roll up the section of quilt on the right as you feed it through.

free motion quilting

Spend time practicing and experimenting to discover
the machine speed and quilt movement that is most comfortable for you.

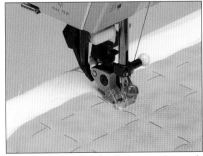

1. Disengage the feed dog and attach a darning foot or special quilting foot. Lock the threads using your chosen method (see previous page).

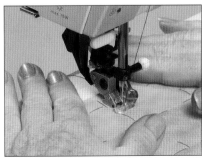

2. As you stitch, hold the fabric with both hands held flat and encircling the needle.

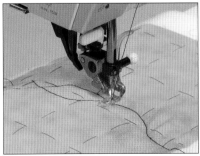

3. Maintaining a steady speed, smoothly move the quilt in the desired directions with your hands.

straight line quilting

Plan the route your quilting will take to minimise the number of times you need to end off the thread.

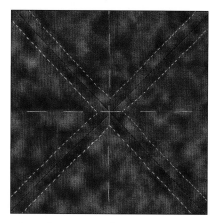

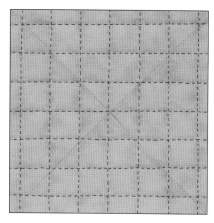

Quilting in the ditch

This is an excellent way to stabilize your quilt. If using this method, it should be completed before continuing with any other quilting.

Stitch in the seamlines around and within the pieced blocks.

Outline quilting

Stitch alongside the seam lines around and within the blocks. Take care to keep the stitching the same distance from the seamlines at all times.

Grid quilting

Working backwards and forwards across the fabric, stitch all the lines in one direction keeping them evenly spaced. When these are complete, stitch all lines at 90° to the first set of lines.

Quilting by machine

Always use a new needle for each new quilting project.

If possible, have the surface of your sewing machine's feed dog level with the surrounding table. This will help reduce drag and the quilt will feed through more evenly.

Place a second table to the left of your chair, butting it up against the sewing machine table to form an L-shape. This will help support the quilt as you stitch.

Ensure the walking foot of your sewing machine is attached or engaged. This will help keep the layers together as they move below the needle.

Whenever you stop stitching, always ensure the needle is in the down position.

Quilt the longest lines first and then fill in with the shorter lines of stitching.

Ensure that the section of the quilt in front of and to the sides of the needle is always smooth and flat.

If your hands do not seem to be holding the quilt firmly enough, wear cotton gloves with rubber tips on the fingers for added grip.

Always work a test sample to check stitch length and tension before stitching on your quilt.

blocking

1. Fold the excess batting and lining over the quilt top and hand baste in place.

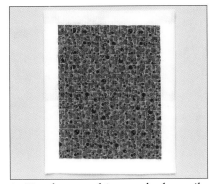

2. Hand or machine wash the quilt. Carefully lay out the damp quilt on a carpeted floor covered with sheets (or similar flat surface). Remove the basting threads and smooth out the quilt with your hands.

3. Using a metal tape measure, measure the length of the quilt through the centre and along each side. Stretch or ease the sides to match the centre measurement.

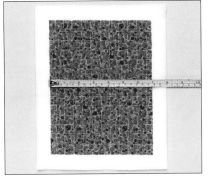

4. Repeat step 3 across the width of the quilt.

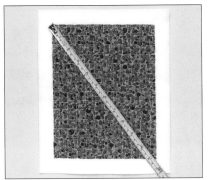

5. Measure diagonally across the quilt from corner to corner. Tug on the corners until the measurement is identical across both diagonals.

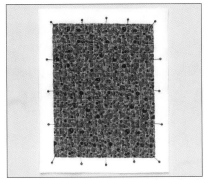

6. Smooth the corners so they look square. Leave the quilt to dry. If required, pin the edges of the quilt to the floor to ensure it remains in place.

squaring

1. Using a large square ruler and using the outermost border seam as an additional guide, line up two adjacent sides of the quilt. Rule lines to mark the straight edges of the quilt.

2. Change to a long straight ruler and continue marking in the same manner along the sides. Continue in the same manner around the entire quilt top.

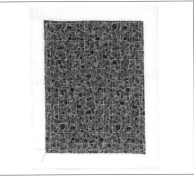

3. Engage the walking foot on your machine and stitch a row of machine basting along the marked line around the entire quilt. Ensure the needle is down each time you pivot. The quilt is now ready for binding.

attaching doubled binding with butted corners

1. Cut the binding strips four times the desired finished width plus 2.5cm (1"). With wrong sides together, fold the strips in half along the length and press.

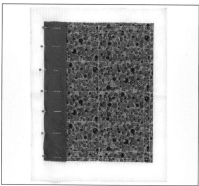

2. Place one side binding on the quilt so the raw edges of the binding are aligned with the raw edge of the quilt top. Pin in place.

3. Stitch in place.

4. Measure out the finished width of the binding from the seamline. Trim away the excess batting and lining fabric beyond this measurement.

5. Press the binding away from the quilt top.

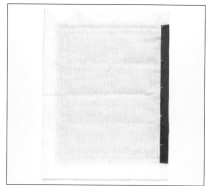

6. Fold the binding to the back. Pin in place so the folded edge of the binding just covers the stitchline.

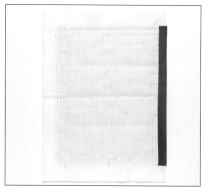

7. Using thread to match the binding, hand stitch the binding to the lining. Do not take the stitches through to the front of the quilt.

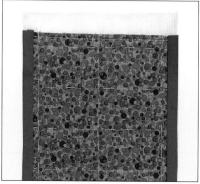

8. Attach the binding to the opposite side in the same manner.

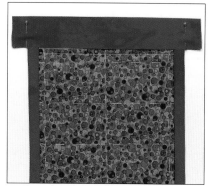

9. Cut the upper binding strip 5cm (2") longer than the width of the quilt top plus side binding pieces. Mark the strip 2.5cm (1") in from each end.

attaching doubled binding with butted corners / continued

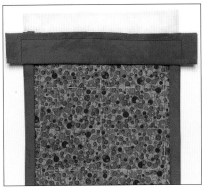

10. Matching raw edges and aligning the marks with the finished sides of the quilt, pin and stitch the strip to the right side of the quilt. Stitch across the ends of the binding as well.

11. Trim the ends of the binding to 1cm (³/₈") beyond the stitching. Trim away the excess batting and lining as before.

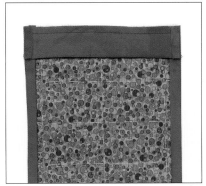

12. Press in the seam allowance at the ends along the stitchlines.

13. Press the binding away from the quilt top as before.

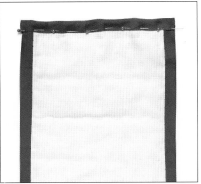

14. Fold the binding to the back. Pin in place so the folded edge of the binding just covers the stitchline.

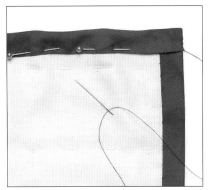

15. Handstitch the folded ends of the binding together at one end.

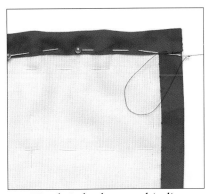

16. Handstitch the top binding to the side binding.

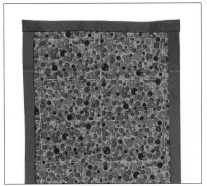

17. Continue stitching the binding to the lining and the remaining folded end. Do not take the stitches through to the front of the quilt.

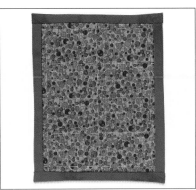

18. Attach the binding to the opposite end in the same manner.

attaching doubled binding with mitred corners

1. Cut the binding strips four times the desired finished width plus 2.5cm (1"). Join the strips to make one continuous length. With wrong sides together, fold the strip in half along the length and press.

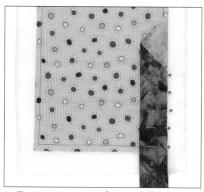

2. Beginning near the middle on one side, pin the binding along this side to the first corner. Keep the raw edges of the binding and quilt top aligned.

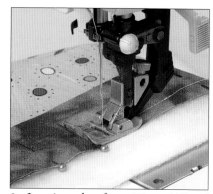

3. Leaving the first 15cm (6") of pinned binding unstitched, begin stitching to the corner.

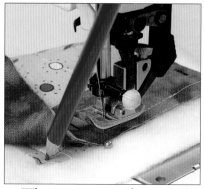

4. When approximately 5cm (2") from the corner, stop with the needle in the down position. Raise the presser foot, turn back the edge of the binding and mark the quilt top where the stitchlines meet at the corner.

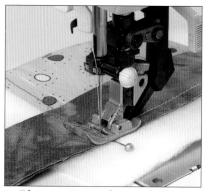

5. Place a pin at the marked spot. Continue stitching until reaching the pin. End off the thread.

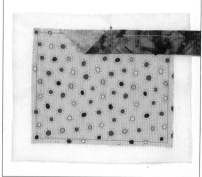

6. Remove the quilt from the machine and turn it so the stitching is at the top.

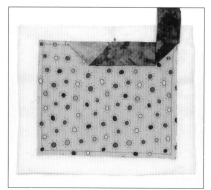

7. Fold the binding strip up at a 45° angle. Press.

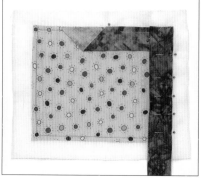

8. Fold the strip down along the adjacent side of the quilt top, aligning raw edges as before. Hold the fold in place with a pin. Pin the strip to the quilt in the same manner as before.

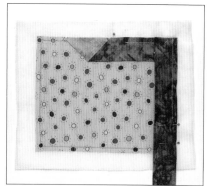

9. Beginning exactly at the fold, stitch until approximately 5cm (2") from the next corner.

attaching doubled binding with mitred corners / continued

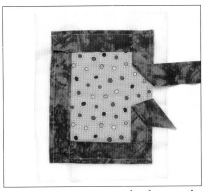

10. Continue around the quilt, forming the corners and stitching until approximately 20cm (8") from where you first started stitching.

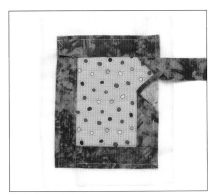

11. Turn under a 6mm (¹/₄") seam allowance at the beginning of the binding strip and press.

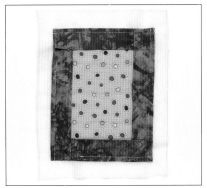

12. Overlay the end of the strip. Leaving a 2cm (³/₄") overlap, trim away any excess binding.

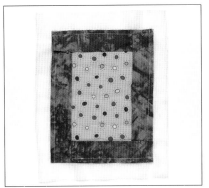

13. Pin and stitch the remaining section of binding in place.

14. Measure out the finished width of the binding from the seamline. Trim away the excess batting and lining fabric beyond this measurement.

15. Press the binding away from the quilt top.

16. Fold the binding to the back and press again. Pin the binding in place. Pin the mitres on the back of the quilt.

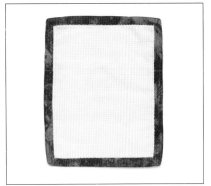

17. Using thread to match the binding, hand stitch the binding to the lining. Do not take the stitches through to the front of the quilt.

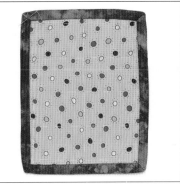

18. Hand stitch the mitres in place.

The A-Z Series

Over 2.2 million sold worldwide.
The ultimate reference books for needleworkers
with amazing projects, detailed step-by-step
instructions and stunning photography.

A-Z of Embroidery Stitches

A-Z of Bullions

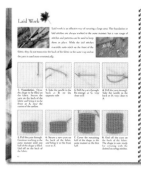

A-Z of Smocking

A-Z of Wool Embroidery

A-Z of Embroidered Flowers

A-Z of Ribbon Embroidery

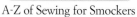

A-Z of Sewing for Smockers

A-Z of Crewel Embroidery

A-Z of Stumpwork

A-Z of Quilting

A-Z of Needlepoint

A-Z of Thread Painting

A-Z of Bead Embroidery

Quarterly Magazines

Filled with beautiful projects, easy instructions, superb photography and full size patterns.

Inspirations

Australian Smocking & Embroidery

Needlework Books

Filled with beautiful projects, easy instructions, superb photography and full size patterns.

Inspirations Gifts

Inspirations Baby

Inspirations Bridal

The World's Most Beautiful Blankets

Embroidered Christening Gowns

The Embroiderer's Handbook

Embroidered Bags and Purses

The Embroidered Village Bag

country bumpkin

For more information on any title, or to place an order, contact Country Bumpkin:

PHONE +61 8 8372 7600

FAX +61 8 8372 7601

EMAIL
mailorder@countrybumpkin.com.au

WEBSITE
www.countrybumpkin.com.au

The Embroidered Patchwork Bear

Beautiful Bishops

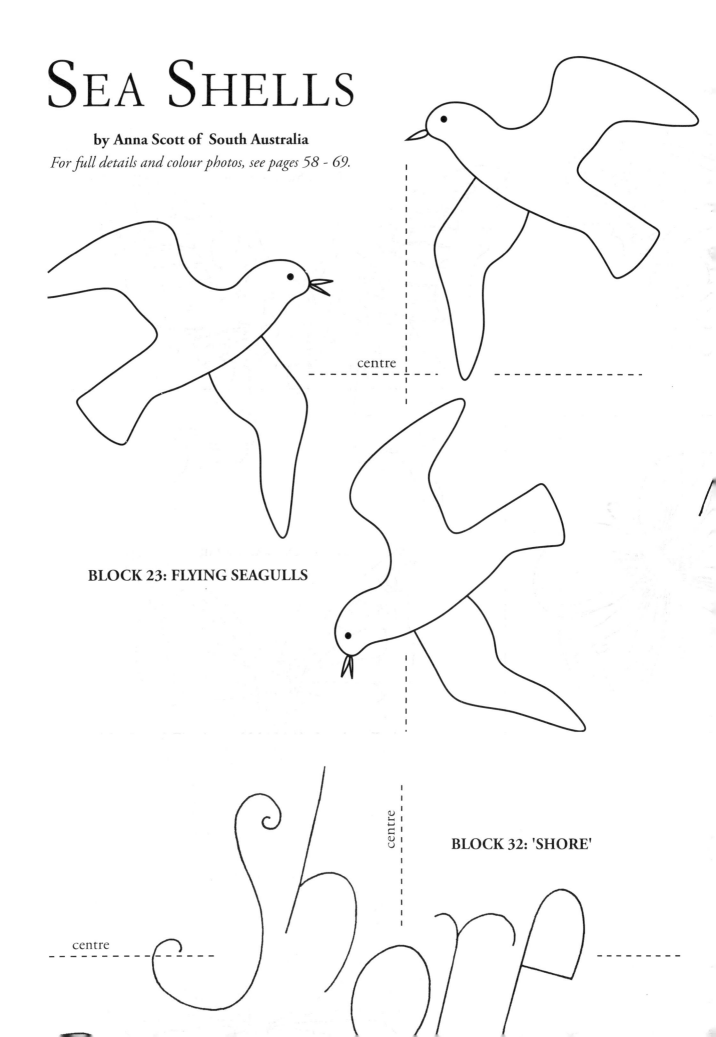

SEA SHELLS

by Anna Scott of South Australia

For full details and colour photos, see pages 58 - 69.

centre

BLOCK 23: FLYING SEAGULLS

centre

BLOCK 32: 'SHORE'

centre

centre

BLOCK 25: 'THE'

BLOCK 29: SEA SNAILS

centre